THE REMINISCENCES OF
John B. Buescher

INTERVIEWED BY
Dr. John T. Mason, Jr.

U.S. Naval Institute • Annapolis, Maryland

Copyright © 2003

Preface

A number of years ago, a naval officer named Geoffrey Wilson recommended to my predecessor, Dr. John T. Mason, Jr., that a colleague of his, Dick Buescher, would be a worthy subject for a Naval Institute oral history. Dr. Mason agreed, and the following interviews ensued. It is my considerable regret that I never had the opportunity to know Mr. Buescher personally, for his record is surely a distinguished one. The number of awards he received and the sense of discipline and quality control that he speaks of in these interviews attest to his record of achievement.

A key contributor to the U.S. victory over the Soviet Union in the long Cold War was the certain knowledge of America's ability to deliver an overwhelming reaction to any nuclear weapons attack against this country. In the eulogy included in this volume, Mr. Buescher's son speaks of a great irony—that his father had created a weapon so terrible that it would be at its most effective if never used in anger. Nuclear deterrence has been an effective shield for the United States ever since the first Polaris-armed submarines went to sea more than 40 years ago. The nuclear peace in those years is a large part of Dick Buescher's legacy to his country.

In the transcript from the oral interviews, Mr. Buescher and I have done some minor editing in the interests of clarity and smoothness, and I have added footnotes and an index for the benefit of readers. Ms. Ann Hassinger of the Naval Institute's history division has made a significant contribution through her diligence in the overall process of printing, proofreading, and overseeing the binding of the completed volumes.

Paul Stillwell

Paul Stillwell
Director, History Division
U.S. Naval Institute
April 2003

John Benedict "Dick" Buescher

Born: 29 November 1919

Parents: Paul Buescher and Ella (Semmes) Buescher

Married: Ann Elizabeth "Betty" Howard

Children: Ann Buescher (m. Haldeman) aka Siri Gian Khalsa
John Benedict Buescher, Jr.

Died: 26 September 1997

Education:

1925-36	St. Aloysius Academy, Meridian, Mississippi
1936-37	Meridian High School, Meridian, Mississippi
1937-38	Meridian Junior College, Meridian, Mississippi
1938-41	Mississippi State College, State College, Mississippi (BS in mechanical engineering)
1967	Harvard University, Cambridge, Massachusetts, Graduate School of Business Administration, Advanced Management Program

Employment:

1941	Alabama Drydock and Shipbuilding Company, Mobile, Alabama
1941-58	Bureau of Ordnance, Navy Department, Washington, D.C.
1958-81	Special Projects Office/Strategic Systems Project Office, Navy Department, Arlington, Virginia

Awards:

1976, 1971, 1980	Department of the Navy Distinguished Civilian Service Award
1969	National Civil Service League Career Service Award
1977	Strategic Systems Projects Office, Merit Award
1980	Navy Unit Citation
1981	Secretary of Defense Meritorious Civilian Service Award
1982	American Institute of Aeronautics and Astronautics, Missile Systems Award

Eulogy

To speak as a son, I offer my father thanks for the life he gave me. To speak for his family, we offer him thanks for the love he gave us. And again, to speak for his family, we offer all of you our thanks for being here today.

Each day, as I was growing up, and I was putting on my white shirt and blue tie, getting ready to come here to St. James for school, my father, like many other fathers, put on a suit, and drove to his office. But unlike many other fathers, when he got to his office, he passed through steel vaulted doors, and went down into the valley of the shadow of death, and there he wrestled the nuclear demon.

My father was the chief engineer for the Navy's nuclear missile submarine project, which designed, built, and deployed the Polaris, Poseidon, and Trident missiles and the nuclear submarines that have carried them. He and his colleagues were brilliantly successful: America's fleet of Trident submarines remains on patrol today, and makes up the major part of our strategic nuclear forces.

I want to be clear about what I meant when I just said he wrestled the nuclear demon: The beautiful weapon he created, he had to make devilishly effective, but it had to never be used. The entire logic behind the submarines and the nuclear missiles they carry is to deter an adversary from launching an attack, because such an attack would be met with a certain and overwhelming counterattack. I therefore repeat now my father's hope and prayer, the one he based his life's work on—May his weapon never be used, May we continue to keep the nuclear demon at bay, May we sense a bright angel of peace, stirring somewhere in the darkness and the secrets in which he struggled, the secret and mysterious darkness that finally greets us all.

My father was an engineer, a supremely practical man. He was a kind and honorable man, too, of strong faith, devoted to his family, a loving father and husband, and sociable, in a thoroughly Southern way, with a constant and gentle sense of humor that overlay a bedrock of strong will. I think his family and colleagues would agree that he was good at being in charge, and that he didn't often hesitate to exercise that ability. He left a legacy, too, in the lives of the boys of this parish as a scout leader. Sometimes I come across small, secret signs that continue to point to his time with the troop: Each year at Christmas, I notice, as I drive by the parish parking lot, the troop still sells Christmas trees, just as we started doing thirty-five years ago. And, to display the trees, the troop still uses the same wooden stands my father built.

I offer you his life as one of integrity. And by that, I mean, it all of one piece. He loved his work, and he was good at it. It was almost as if he was born to be an engineer—he had a fine appreciation of function and form, and took a real joy in creating things that worked. And, in hindsight, his interest in trajectories and ballistics went back into his childhood: One of his brothers remembered recently how, as a boy, Dick made the most effective rubber-band pistols in the neighborhood, out of rings sliced from automobile inner tubes, and that Dick spent a long time perfecting the art of skipping stones on water.

That boy is the Dick Buescher who wound up engineering the development of the Polaris, and then Poseidon, and then Trident missiles. There was innovative genius in the project, and Dad managed and made use of that genius.

Just one example of his engineering team's unusual creativity—Working on one generation of Poseidon missile, they found stresses on the rigid metal used for the casing of the missile. They looked for some other material to use instead, that had more "give" to it. The composite materials we have today were not around then, but the team did find something: They hit on the idea of building the missile out Sitka Spruce—like some kind of kid's airplane model. They created the world's most advanced missile, and it came out looking like a long wooden barrel. And it worked. Other engineering teams in the government and in industry have almost never achieved the kinds of success they did. And it was certainly for that reason, that Dad was asked to serve as an advisor to the commission that reviewed the engineering design of the Space Shuttle after the Challenger disaster.

When he retired, his colleagues commissioned a carved, wooden, Red-tailed Hawk for him as a gift. The inscription on its pedestal said, "From your many friends and associates whom you have watched like a hawk for years." He and Mom often took binoculars out to the woods to watch eagles and hawks. They and my sister were even planning an expedition out to the mountains a couple of days ago to watch the hawks migrating.

My father had his own rare inner strength and intensity of purpose, and admired that same steadfastness in hawks, and admired, too, the way they shaped and bent their form and design into an arc of single winged purpose.

I don't really know how to measure the significance of a person's life for the rest of us, but it seems to me that Dad's work has had, and will continue to have, immense consequences for every human being on this planet. He would never have said that—As I said, he was a practical man with a sense of humor about himself, and not given to speculating about his own importance. He merely went down every day into the watery depths and, in the dark there, wrestled the demon that has haunted our Age. And he did that for us. And in that was his integrity.

He taught his children to find the North Star, Polaris, fixed and bright, something singular and steady you can set your sights on. The integrity of his own life was unswerving, too, but it had its own trajectory through the dark, and that trajectory was a bright arc of love and duty, faith and joy. Let us then be grateful for that joy, and share it with one another, as he shared it with us.

John B. Buescher, Jr.
September 29, 1997

DECLARATION OF TRUST

The undersigned does hereby appoint and designate as his (her) Trustee herein, the Secretary-Treasurer and Publisher of the United States Naval Institute to perform and discharge the following duties, powers, and privileges in connection with the possession and use of a certain taped interview between the undersigned and the Oral History Department of the United States Naval Institute.

1. Classification of Transcript.

    (√)a. If classified OPEN, the transcript(s) may be read or the recording(s) audited by the qualified personnel upon presentation of proper credentials, as determined by the Secretary-Treasurer of the U.S. Naval Institute.

    ( )b. If classified PERMISSION REQUIRED TO CITE OR QUOTE, the user will be required to obtain permission in writing from the interviewee prior to quoting or citing from either the transcript(s) or the recording(s).

    ( )c. If classified PERMISSION REQUIRED, permission must be obtained in writing from the interviewee before the transcribed interview(s) can be examined or the tape recording(s) audited.

    ( )d. If classified CLOSED, the transcribed interview(s) and the tape recording(s) will be sealed until a time specified by the interviewee. This may be until the death of the interviewee or for any specified number of years.

2. It is expressly understood that in giving this authorization, I am in no way precluded from placing such restrictions as I may desire upon use of the interview at any time during my lifetime, nor does this authorization in any way affect my rights to the copyright of my literary expressions that may be contained in the interview.

Witness my hand and seal this 15 day of May 1982.

John B. Buescher

I hereby accept and consent to the foregoing Declaration of Trust and the powers therein conferred upon me as Trustee:

R.T.E. Bowler Jr
5/24/'82

Interview Number 1 with Mr. John B. Buescher

Place: Mr. Buescher's residence in Falls Church, Virginia

Date: Tuesday, 17 November 1981

Interviewer: John T. Mason, Jr.

John T. Mason, Jr.: Well, I have looked forward to this for several months now since we made our initial engagement. As I just told you, this is a talking biography, so today perhaps you'll give me some background to your ultimate achievement with the Special Projects operation in the Navy.* Would you begin by telling me where you were born and when you were born and something about your family background and your early education?

Mr. Buescher: I was born in Brookhaven, Mississippi, in 1919 and later moved to Meridian, Mississippi, where I spent most of my life up through college.

John T. Mason, Jr.: Your father, what business was he in?

Mr. Buescher: First he was a farmer; then a general construction foreman; and later manager of a dairy processing plant. He came from Germany in 1909.

John T. Mason, Jr.: I thought there was a German ancestry, from the name.

Mr. Buescher: Yes. My mother was born and raised in Meridian, Mississippi. After they were married, they went to Brookhaven, Mississippi, because he had bought some acreage down there—700 or 800 acres. Then later they moved back to Meridian.

---

* Over the years the Special Projects Office, often referred to by only the initials SP, managed the U.S. Navy's submarine-launched ballistic missile programs. The name of the organization was changed in July 1968 to Strategic Systems Project Office; in March 1984 to Strategic Systems Program Office; and in December 1987 to the current name, Strategic Systems Programs.

John T. Mason, Jr.: And you went to the public schools there, did you?

Mr. Buescher: I went for 11 years to the Catholic school, and then my last year I went to the public school and graduated at Meridian High School. From there I went to Meridian Junior College for one year and then—

John T. Mason, Jr.: The junior college must have been a relatively new establishment, wasn't it?

Mr. Buescher: I'm surprised you said that, because the year I went was the first year they had one. Then the last three years I went to Mississippi State College, and I got a B.S. in mechanical engineering.

John T. Mason, Jr.: Is that in Jackson?

Mr. Buescher: That's in Starkville, Mississippi. I graduated in 1941.

John T. Mason, Jr.: By that time you had determined to be an engineer?

Mr. Buescher: I had my bachelor's degree in engineering.

John T. Mason, Jr.: What led you in that direction?

Mr. Buescher: Oh, I don't know what leads people to do things. It just seemed very interesting.

John T. Mason, Jr.: You must have had some aptitude also.

Mr. Buescher: I was interested in things like diesel engines and things of that sort, although I've never worked with diesel engines since I graduated. When I graduated, I went to work for a shipyard, the Alabama Dry Dock and Shipbuilding Company in Mobile.

John T. Mason, Jr.: What kind of work did you do there?

Mr. Buescher: Well, they were just getting organized for the war effort, and although they had contracts for larger ships like the Liberty ships and other big cargo and tanker ships, at that time we were building tugs.* We were planning and organizing that effort and getting that going. I was there the summer before I got the offer from Washington to come up and work in the Navy's Bureau of Ordnance.

John T. Mason, Jr.: You had applied for Civil Service status, did you?

Mr. Buescher: Yes.

John T. Mason, Jr.: Had you taken the examination?

Mr. Buescher: They didn't require any exam at that time. They called it an open exam and didn't require a written exam. So I came on up to Washington and went into the design section of the Bureau of Ordnance. At that time the Bureau of Ordnance, the Washington group, did its own design. Over the years since World War II, the Navy—BuOrd, BuWeps, NavSea—in order to get more diversified help, has gradually gone out on contract for that type of support.† It has become more a management rather than a design organization. I just think that's certainly for the better of the Navy.

John T. Mason, Jr.: You think it is good development?

Mr. Buescher: In the government you're always restricted more by billets than by money.

---

* The Liberty ship was a mass-produced cargo ship designed by the U.S. Maritime Commission for use by the Allies in World War II. All told, American shipyards built 2,770 Liberties. The standard Liberty was 442 feet long, 57 feet in the beam, and had a light displacement of 3,337 tons. It had a cargo capacity of 10,920 deadweight tons.
† BuOrd, the Bureau of Ordnance existed until 1959, when it was combined with the Bureau of Aeronautics to form the Bureau of Naval Weapons (BuWeps). In 1966 there was a split that separated out the former BuOrd as the Naval Ordnance Systems Command (NavOrd). In 1974 NavOrd was merged with the Naval Ship Systems Command to form the Naval Sea Systems Command (NavSea), which exists to the present.

By being able to pull on contractors for all types of expertise, you can bring the help and experience in and out of programs.

John T. Mason, Jr.: More flexibility.

Mr. Buescher: A lot more flexibility. It's just a much better arrangement, as long as you've got good people in the government to control it. You don't have to look over their shoulders, but you do the key elements of getting it managed and getting it managed right and applying your money where it ought to be. It's important that you are very careful, when you put your money out on contract, that you follow the effort in sufficient degree that you know what your specifications are, and that you are working with them to come up to the needed results.

John T. Mason, Jr.: Doesn't that mean, however, that it's more expensive to have that system with the managerial part in the bureau?

Mr. Buescher: Not necessarily. Particularly with a big project like the Polaris and the Poseidon, you couldn't have gotten that number of people to do the job and have done it right.[*]

John T. Mason, Jr.: Yes, that's a shining example of the merit of what you're talking about.

Mr. Buescher: Tremendous facilities are required by the R&D phase and the production phase.[†] You've got to have somebody that can back you up and can provide these things as well as the expertise, not just in your program, but in bringing in knowledge from all other programs too. This hiring and firing bit and the billet—and whether or not Congress is going to cut you on billets this year or next year—makes it very difficult to try to keep small. At least we in SP did in our project; we tried to keep small and flexible and light on our feet and work and keep things moving, rather than try to do all of it ourselves. That

---

[*] Polaris was the U.S. Navy's first submarine-launched ballistic missile, which became operational in the early 1960s. Its more-capable follow-on was the Poseidon missile, which entered the fleet in 1970.
[†] R&D—research and development.

has worked just great, just absolutely great for us.

John T. Mason, Jr.: I suppose if the government system were more flexible, it would work all in one place, wouldn't it?

Mr. Buescher: Well, if it's more flexible, yes. There's no reason why you couldn't draw people if flexible in salary, flexible in hiring and firing, and flexible in terms of being able to go out and use many billets. You see, industry is not billet limited; government is. Kind of off the subject, but this is one reason we found it difficult to extensively use government facilities, laboratories, in our development program. It was very difficult for government facilities to make a commitment which they could be sure to carry out regularly—their commitment on how many people they were going to put and retain on your program. Secondly, that they would build facilities, because Congress has got to get involved, rather deeply. You don't have the flexibility in the government building program that you have in the contracting.

John T. Mason, Jr.: No, you have the GAO looking over your shoulder.[*]

Mr. Buescher: I'm not in any way implying that we went around anything. This was strictly within all rules and regulations, but I believe this was a factor in our decisions not to expressly utilize government facilities in building laboratories, although we would have liked very much to do so. In a direct sense, what we did, we used them as experts to advise and back us up, rather than giving them the big job of doing it. And that worked out very fine. They were a very important and integral part of our program but in a different sense; we didn't give them the primarily development job to do.

John T. Mason, Jr.: In that time, when you came up to Washington in the early '40s to work with the government, did we have many outside organizations in existence as we seem to have now?

---

[*] GAO—General Accounting Office.

John B. Buescher, Interview #1 (11/17/81) – Page 6

Mr. Buescher: You mean contractors?

John T. Mason, Jr.: Yes, think-tank outfits.

Mr. Buescher: Not think tanks. That's come about since World War II, to a great extent. You had some of it. Let's see, I came up to Washington in July, and by December we were in the war, you see.* So it was a wartime situation.

John T. Mason, Jr.: It certainly was. All of that year was wartime.
   What was your specific job in ordnance?

Mr. Buescher: Well, when I first reported, I was involved in the design of gun mounts, aircraft guns, shipboard guns. Then I moved over to the ammunition group in which we handled gun ammunition and later on rocket developments and design. When I'm talking about gun ammunition, I'm talking about cartridge cases, fuzes that go on the front of a projectile, containers for these things. As a matter of fact, my biggest job during the war was the design of gun and rocket fuzes. After World War II our major efforts were on aircraft, bombardment and antisubmarine rocket design and developments, and still later on guided missiles.

John T. Mason, Jr.: Did you work with Dr. Tuve, the VT fuze?†

Mr. Buescher: No, I didn't, I personally didn't. It wasn't until after World War II that I got involved in VT fuzes. We did work with people at Naval Rocket Test Station; the Navy's rocket design group. All the bombardment rockets and all later rockets, the aircraft rockets and shipboard rockets, came out of there. We were working with a number of people and activities like NOL White Oak, MPG Dahlgren, NOTS Inyokern with gun ammunition,

---

* Japanese naval aircraft attacked the U.S. Fleet in Pearl Harbor, Hawaii, on Sunday, 7 December 1941. Congress declared war on Japan the following day.
† Dr. Merle A. Tuve was instrumental in the development of the proximity fuze for 5-inch antiaircraft projectiles. It was also known as the VT, or variable time fuze. For a detailed account, see Buford Bowland and William R. Boyd, U.S. Navy Bureau of Ordnance in World War II (Washington, D.C.: U.S. Government Printing Office, 1953), pages 271-290.

because these were established programs, whereas the rocket program was something new that came in just during and after World War II.[*]

I guess we did two things. We did design work, and we also did production engineering and design control during production. We found one thing: that most of these equipments' designs, when released by the laboratories like NOL White Oak, would have been design-tested, but they would not have been designed for high-rate production. We would take those designs and production-engineer them, acting as a design control group and controlling all changes.

John T. Mason, Jr.: And you worked with industry, then?

Mr. Buescher: We were the interface with industry. The government laboratories had the experimental design drawings. We'd take them and convert them to production-engineered designs and then act as the technical group working with the Bureau of Ordnance procurement group.

John T. Mason, Jr.: You weren't hamstrung at that point by bids, were you?

Mr. Buescher: No.

John T. Mason, Jr.: This was direct arrangement.

Mr. Buescher: We had a production group in the Bureau of Ordnance who procured all this ammunition in quantity. We happened to be working with the ammunition production group, and they'd go out on contracts and find people to develop sources of production. You know, you converted shoe factories to make gun mounts and converted a little die cast shop to make critical parts in the fuze. The production group would develop all these production sources, and we were working to support them yet retaining the responsibility as design agent.

---

[*] NOL—Naval Ordnance Laboratory, White Oak, Maryland; NPG—Naval Proving Ground, Dahlgren, Virginia; NOTS—Naval Ordnance Test Station, Inyokern, California.

John T. Mason, Jr.: Can you recall some specific experiences with industry?

Mr. Buescher: Well, just take a cartridge case. You're making cartridge cases. We worked from the 20-millimeter size up to 8-inch size cartridge cases. It had always been a black art; there wasn't much to go on, how they had been making them always before. Why they did or didn't work was in somebody's head. We finally got the production design down to a pretty scientific thing and spelled it out carefully so as to understand what was going on, working with industry to help us come up with what we'd need. What was different was that we were going to higher gun pressures and longer-range and high-velocity guns. That had the effect on cartridge cases' ability to take the expansion in a gun and then to be able to be ejected.

John T. Mason, Jr.: What specific company or companies did you work with directly?

Mr. Buescher: Norris Thermolab on the West Coast in L.A. Echo Products was another one. We worked with a number of companies in the fuze business. I don't remember all these people, people like Edison, on the clockwork fuzes, Raytheon, Eastman Kodak. There must have been 15 or 20, because they were producing these items so fast in such large quantities and needed big production plants. These were the fuzes and ammunition components used for many different sizes of guns.

John T. Mason, Jr.: I think Westclox was working in that area.

Mr. Buescher: Yes, Westclox was working, and I really have forgotten all these companies. The BuOrd production group was primarily in charge of these contracts. Some of these plants were temporary to do these wartime jobs and were closed after the end of the war. Some of them were built just for this; some of them were a subsidiary of a larger company.

John T. Mason, Jr.: Did the government assist some of these companies to build themselves up to handle these contracts?

Mr. Buescher: I'm sure they did, although I was in the R&D side of it and not the production side. But they did anything they could to help it go during the war.

John T. Mason, Jr.: That whole total story is a fabulous one.

Mr. Buescher: It really is.

John T. Mason, Jr.: I got some of that. Was George Hussey head of the bureau in those days?*

Mr. Buescher: Yes.

John T. Mason, Jr.: I know George very well and I got some of that from him, the idea then of the big story on VT fuze.

Mr. Buescher: The VT fuze came along. As a matter of fact, after the war the program was moved out of APL into our branch, in our fuze section. During the war the VT fuze program was in a special group set up at APL/JHU.†

John T. Mason, Jr.: Yes, and it was one of those secret things—almost like radar, it was so secret.

Mr. Buescher: Right after the war, the whole VT fuze effort was brought in under our branch, RE-2; that's just a branch with a number for management control. And it was still a pretty controlled thing, security wise. But it was very interesting.

---

* Rear Admiral George F. Hussey, USN, became Chief of the Bureau of Ordnance in 1943, was promoted to vice admiral in 1945, and remained in the billet until 1947. Dr. Mason interviewed Admiral Hussey for the Columbia University oral history program.
† APL/JHU—Applied Physics Laboratory, Johns Hopkins University.

John T. Mason, Jr.: Was radar a problem in BuOrd at that time?

Mr. Buescher: BuOrd was developing and producing radar.

John T. Mason, Jr.: Those were hectic times. Tell me, was Red Schoeffel there?[*]

Mr. Buescher: Oh, yes. Schoeffel, a very fine guy. Hussey and Schoeffel were the main two I worked with, and there were a couple others during my time.

John T. Mason, Jr.: That was a very interesting period. How long were you with BuOrd then?

Mr. Buescher: From 1941 through 1956, although it was known as BuWeps at the time I left in 1956.

John T. Mason, Jr.: You were there during the whole period of World War II?

Mr. Buescher: Yes. As a matter of fact, during one period of that time, RE-2 was a branch, ammunitions and explosives. After the war Commander Levering Smith was in RE-2D in our branch.[†]

John T. Mason, Jr.: Oh, he was?

Mr. Buescher: Yes, he was in the rocket propellant program, I guess, '41 to '47. That's when we broke up the design group and went into more management groups. I was there as a project engineer from '47 to '53. Then I moved up to branch engineer and stayed there until late '56. Then I moved to SP as chief engineer in December 1956 to work on

---

[*] Rear Admiral Malcolm F. Schoeffel, USN, served as Chief of the Bureau of Ordnance, 1950-54. His oral history is in the Naval Institute collection.
[†] Commander Levering Smith, USN. Smith later had an instrumental role in the submarine-launched ballistic missile program, which Mr. Buescher describes in detail in this oral history.

the Polaris FBM program.*

John T. Mason, Jr.: And right on up the ladder. Well, let's go back again.

Mr. Buescher: In that period in BuOrd I really learned what it was all about. You come out of college, and you don't know too much.

John T. Mason, Jr.: You know the theories.

Mr. Buescher: You know the theories. I really got my hands into things and learned what programs were, how to run programs. The phases went from R&D to development, to testing, to production, and then maintenance. I had a good opportunity to see many things, not just in our group, but other groups that did work. A lot of great things got accomplished. When things didn't succeed, often it was due to the fact that technically it wasn't feasible, because they were pushing the state of the art. Sometimes it was simply because the effort was not properly managed. You find that in government; you also find that in industry.

John T. Mason, Jr.: The theory is good.

Mr. Buescher: The theory is good, but if you don't do your job, the total job right, it can go down the drain, particularly with weapon systems. They're different, say, from an automobile, where you have a lot of outlets. There you take the product back into the shop for repair, and there are a lot of shops around to do the repair. With a weapon system the Navy turns over a weapon system to a unique set of guys, the sailors, who have to be specifically trained. You have to keep them on the job long enough to keep the continuity; you have to do all these things right. Each ship has to have repair parts support and capability to operate and maintain very complex systems. The ship can't run out to the corner shop to get it done. The effectiveness of the system goes down if you didn't train the guys right; you don't give them the spare parts; you don't give them the right

---

* FBM—fleet ballistic missile.

documentation and support. If the Navy doesn't do its job right, one can see it all falling apart.

John T. Mason, Jr.: If you're really discerning.

Mr. Buescher: Yes. You can see it happening. You may not understand why it's happening, but most of the time it's that same thing; somebody hasn't done the right planning, hasn't provided the proper support, or somebody hasn't done the right job looking downstream.

John T. Mason, Jr.: You really can't coordinate it to the point—

Mr. Buescher: You can coordinate it, and that's one of the things SP has done; it has kept the whole job, the whole life-cycle management. But it was a big help to me in the early years to see and understand why things happened so this could be applied later on. It provided an excellent experience training and background for my work in the Polaris program.

John T. Mason, Jr.: It certainly was essential, wasn't it? And a rare opportunity, I would say.

Mr. Buescher: A rare opportunity, because in SP we started from scratch. We didn't have to do it like anybody else had been doing it over the years. We could do it our own way, and that's a rare opportunity. You don't get many opportunities in a lifetime to do it that way.

John T. Mason, Jr.: No, you don't. But you don't get many opportunities to learn at the level you learned, either, under the duress of war. You must have had some good mentors, however, at that point.

Mr. Buescher: Yes, good people. I worked for good people.

John T. Mason, Jr.: Can you mention some of them?

Mr. Buescher: Yes. I learned a lot from my immediate bosses. I came in the fuze business and I worked for a guy that only I, perhaps, remember. His name was Milton Sheppa. He ran the fuze group. He was a very meticulous guy. He taught me a lot. He retired many years ago. He in turn worked for a guy named Fred Bitner. We didn't call it this, but these were the early days of my involvement on configuration control. Configuration control involves the changes and modifications to design and the documentation and so forth. So you got a uniform product.

John T. Mason, Jr.: And so they don't get out on a tangent?

Mr. Buescher: That's right, and so you don't have a lot of people making changes. When you go into high-rate production like a fuze or a cartridge case or a primer, you want all those things, no matter who makes them, to be the same. You may have 20 companies making the same item. You want them all to turn out to be the exact same thing so the same high-quality performance can be obtained. You can't do it without good configuration control.

John T. Mason, Jr.: So you were an SP manager right there, weren't you?

Mr. Buescher: Those were my days of learning, you see. The ammunition business was quite different from the gun mount business and other parts of the system. We worked up systems of configuration control and had all producers working from the same set of drawings. Proposed changes or modifications coming back were controlled by the same group. This is what I meant by taking control; don't turn the design over to the production people and let them make it without such technical control, because you'll end up with each producer making a different item because of changes introduced for the convenience of each producer. We acted as the technical control group to ensure there weren't any changes made without our approval, after design recertification and test as necessary.

John T. Mason, Jr.: How long had this wisdom prevailed in the bureau?

Mr. Buescher: Well, Bitner and Sheppa had been around for a number of years. But the bureau probably wasn't producing anything for the last 15 years during peacetime, because the Navy really didn't have any use for additional quantities of these items. They didn't have many ships; they were not really using up quantities on hand. So this was a buildup of development and production capability that began before I reported to BuOrd in 1941. After Pearl Harbor, things really broke loose and moved fast. It wasn't too long before both old and new development items were in full production with millions of the items under production.

John T. Mason, Jr.: Did you feel the pressure from the fleet in your part of the organization?

Mr. Buescher: No, but we felt very responsible for the fleet equipments in terms of the gear we gave to them. You know, for a while the Navy wasn't doing too well in the war, but after a while—after we started having a number victories and winning all these sea battles—we felt we had had a big part. We took considerable pride in our contribution to help give the Navy good material to use out there. We were very conscious of that, as a matter of fact. For instance, I had a brother abroad in the merchant marine; a brother with Patton's Army in the tanks; a brother in the Navy on a destroyer; and a brother-on-law in the Air Force.[*] I was the only one ashore, and I felt I was making my contribution to them. I felt very conscious it had better be a good one, so I was trying very hard.

John T. Mason, Jr.: Did the bureau as a whole learn from the tragedy of the torpedoes?

Mr. Buescher: Which one are you talking about—the tragedy of the torpedoes?

---

[*] George S. Patton became famous as an Army officer in World War II, leading the U.S. Third Army across Europe following the D-Day invasion in 1944. At the time of his death in late 1945 he was a four-star general.

John B. Buescher, Interview #1 (11/17/81) – Page 15

John T. Mason, Jr.: In the early part of the war, when they wouldn't work, wouldn't detonate, wouldn't stay at right level.*

Mr. Buescher: Lack of configuration control was a major factor. They did not have configuration control in those years. Every torpedo was handmade, hand assembled, unique. They didn't know if they'd work or not. You test one, and it wasn't representative of the lot, you see. It wasn't representative of the whole group of torpedoes you had. They were designed so that an awful lot of babying, changing, matching of parts had to be done in the fleet by the sailors. You know, that's a pretty mobile situation, fleet personnel, and you try to keep them up to date on the latest thing. You can't have all these people making changes and expect it to work.

John T. Mason, Jr.: Also, I've talked to a lot of the skippers of submarines, and they were constrained by rules and regulations out of BuOrd. They were not supposed to do anything about it, you see. They did for their salvation.

Mr. Buescher: That's right. But that torpedo problems persisted throughout the war, even ten years after the war; maybe it still does. I've kind of gotten away from it today. They have improved in certain respects, but they just—I don't mean to be critical of them. Maybe they didn't have billets, and maybe they didn't have money to do anything. That could be the key to the whole thing.

John T. Mason, Jr.: They did say from the bureau, I think, that they didn't have the money that they could fuze live warheads in tests.

Mr. Buescher: Throughout the peacetime years the Navy didn't get much money to keep this kind of thing going.

---

* During the early part of World War II, U.S. torpedoes were notorious for running deeper than the designed settings and for malfunctioning or poorly functioning exploders in cases in which the torpedoes did hit their targets. For details see David E. Cohen, "The Mk-XIV Torpedo: Lessons for Today," Naval History, Winter 1992, pages 34-36.

John T. Mason, Jr.: Getting back to my original question about the torpedoes, did the bureau, in a sense, learn from this so that your configuration control was a result, in part, of this?

Mr. Buescher: I don't know how well they learned. I'm too far away today from torpedoes to say that they've got it under control. I suspect they're like most of the other part of the Navy—they don't, not to the degree that SP does.

John T. Mason, Jr.: But I mean in the immediate time when you were there.

Mr. Buescher: They made improvements. They put a lot of effort, a lot of effort trying to bring it up to snuff and spent a lot of money.

John T. Mason, Jr.: So I can see the benefit of what I termed a tragedy—the benefit as it accrued and finally appeared in SP, in the control, in the configuration.

Mr. Buescher: We had very few torpedoes.

John T. Mason, Jr.: I know that, but I mean the whole approach, the technique, the control.

Mr. Buescher: That's right, but we in ammunition programs didn't learn from the torpedo program. In the ammunition business, we had it under control. We had it under control simply because of the guys before me. This is how the business had come up. I learned from them and added what I could to improve the systems.

John T. Mason, Jr.: How much leeway did you have personally, I mean, to add through your analysis of things?

Mr. Buescher: I had all the freedom in the world to analyze changes and things of this sort and to exercise management controls and techniques we felt necessary. We tried very hard to keep changes from being made. Sometimes a new production method—I've mentioned die-casting and things of this sort—came along. We redesigned a number of items to have the pieces die-cast that had previously been machined and hogged out and things of that sort, simply because without doing it, you couldn't get the production of quantities you needed. You needed millions of these things, and you had to get the designs such so there were enough producers around to produce them at a high daily rate, and meet the orders. So we redesigned a number of things for this purpose, and we tested them very thoroughly, too, before we let them go to production. We also developed management controls and techniques to ensure success. I don't know if I've answered your question or not.

John T. Mason, Jr.: I think you have. Now, the testing of the product. This was before OpDevFor came into being, and so what organization was set up to test them?[*]

Mr. Buescher: Oh, we had activities like Naval Proving Ground in Dahlgren, Virginia; Naval Ordnance Test Station in China Lake, California; Naval Ordnance Lab, White Oak; and other government facilities.

John T. Mason, Jr.: Yes, yes, of course you did.

Mr. Buescher: People like this had test facilities. We relied heavily on them. I keep talking about ammunition, which was what I was working; that is a one-shot job. It either works or it doesn't work. You can take some other thing like something that's installed aboard ship and you can run all kinds of tests repeatedly and repeatedly and repeatedly and check out the extremes in different combinations of situations and so forth.

With ammunition, if all that you produced of a certain type was produced with the same design and you could take samples of a lot which was representative of that lot— because it was just like anything else in that—then you could statistically select your samples for testing and get some pretty good idea of what the quality of the lot was. That's what we relied on. You may make a lot of 2,000 or 10,000 in a lot, and then you'd select a certain percentage out of that and run them through the tests. You'd fire at a target, or

---

[*] OpDevFor—Operational Development Force, a group of ships and aircraft used for conducting operational tests of new weapons, systems, and equipment.

you'd shoot against plates or concrete or whatever you chose.

Like in the desert you'd fire these bombardment rockets; you'd determine under varying test conditions how many went off and how many either fired or they didn't fire. Or aircraft ammunition was the same way; you'd take them out and fire at targets, but you were firing representative statistical samples out of a lot. Because you had the designing of the item and the production line under strict control, you knew that lot was uniform.

John T. Mason, Jr.: Did you ever branch out into a sister element, that is, the mines?

Mr. Buescher: No, I never did get in mines. I was involved in ammunition and explosives.

John T. Mason, Jr.: It certainly was a big enough field.

Mr. Buescher: It was a big enough field.

John T. Mason, Jr.: Was it necessary to travel to some of the industries that produced the ammunition? Did you check on the control of the exercise there?

Mr. Buescher: Oh, yes.

John T. Mason, Jr.: Tell me about that.

Mr. Buescher: The Bureau of Ordnance recognized the problem of inspection particularly in the ammunition business, and set up a quality-control division in the Bureau of Ordnance. Commander Lubelsky headed that up; he's now dead.* He set up a group of statisticians, inspectors who really brought the concept of quality control to the BuOrd, and I'm sure that torpedoes had something to do with it. I'm sure that large-scale ammunition production had something to do with it. All of it contributed, you see.

John T. Mason, Jr.: Sometimes in a subtle way.

---

* Commander Benjamin L. Lubelsky, USN.

Mr. Buescher: Yes. And this tied right in with the inspection service, the Office of Naval Material at that time. The Navy inspectors were under them rather than BuOrd at the time.

We were required to go out from time to time and visit each of these factories and see what they were doing, see what the problems were, resolve these problems, and kind of get things squared away when they couldn't solve them.

John T. Mason, Jr.: Gave you a chance to get some fresh air, too, didn't it?

Mr. Buescher: That's right.

John T. Mason, Jr.: Where did you go?

Mr. Buescher: We went all over the country, depending on whoever was designing, developing, testing or producing these items. You'd spend two or three days in different places. Actually, you'd get in there and work with the contractors and with the government inspectors on the line. This whole modern idea of inspection techniques really was created during that wartime period. Of course, configuration control came in. I keep talking about that, if there was a waiver or a deviation to a material that was going to be made, it had to come back to us for review and approval.

John T. Mason, Jr.: You mean the manufacturer said it was necessary in order to—

Mr. Buescher: He'd do that, or he may have made it and had got a lot of material on hand that he would like to use and present to the government for acceptance. But it didn't meet specifications in all respects, so we had to go out and see whether they threw that material away or whether the government could use it. There can be some defects as long as it's not a critical defect, which wouldn't make it unusable.

It may be just the littlest thing, such as whether or not it's got the right radius in a little corner, and that can be very important from the standpoint of stress. Or it could be a stain on it or it could be something much more critical, such as a dimension out of tolerance. It could be pittings in castings, or it could be a request to really change it completely. So we got involved in that type of thing by going out and talking to the companies and talking to the inspectors. We never went out as kind of us against them; it was always a team effort. We also similarly got involved in development programs under our cognizance.

John T. Mason, Jr.: And I suppose, too, that there was a lot of experience coming in from the operators in the fleet and elsewhere that taught you things about metal fatigue and that type of thing.

Mr. Buescher: That's right; it did.

John T. Mason, Jr.: Which the manufacturer wouldn't necessarily know.

Mr. Buescher: No, but we didn't get too much of that. Working with ammunition, you don't get too much fatigue, although you had an overflow from the other people, from gun mounts and things of that sort that would come back. We did get involved in things like gun barrel wear, simply because it was our propellant that was eating them out, a hot propellant. And we would do things to cool the propellants or something to give them the ability to reduce the wear.

John T. Mason, Jr.: Was the gun factory in operation then?

Mr. Buescher: The gun factory was in operation, and I still call it the gun factory, although it was closed and renamed many years ago.[*]

John T. Mason, Jr.: Quite changed now.

Mr. Buescher: Called the Washington Navy Yard now. We worked very closely with

---

[*] The Naval Gun Factory, on M Street in southeast Washington, D.C., for many years manufactured guns for the U.S. Navy. The site has since been renamed the Washington Navy Yard. It contains the offices of a number of commands, as well residences of several active-duty flag officers.

them. They provided very good assistance to help us get things done in a hurry, if we wanted to develop something or try out an idea real fast, they had facilities for turning out whatever it was, metal works and things of that sort.

John T. Mason, Jr.: Was Indian Head in operation?[*]

Mr. Buescher: Yes, Indian Head was and still is. They did a lot of propellant work for us. NOL did our explosive work for us in White Oak, the laboratory.

John T. Mason, Jr.: Going back to the trips to the factories, were they all very cooperative when you insisted on management control of the ammunition? They caved in at that point?

Mr. Buescher: Yes, they were okay; they were trying to get the job done. Of course, you'd find some people who had their feathers ruffled, and you kind of had to work them a little bit, but it all came to everybody trying to get the job done and win the war.

John T. Mason, Jr.: And they all had family connections like yours, so they felt the need.

Mr. Buescher: That's right. That's exactly right.

John T. Mason, Jr.: Where did you live at this point?

Mr. Buescher: I lived in the Washington area all the time.

John T. Mason, Jr.: You were married by that time?

Mr. Buescher: I married in 1943. I lived in some apartments in Arlington County. I moved to Fairfax County during the Korean War.

---

[*] Indian Head, Maryland, was the site of a naval powder factory.

John T. Mason, Jr.: What was transportation like in Arlington County at that point?

Mr. Buescher: Well, it wasn't too bad. They had buses. We lived in Buckingham community.

John T. Mason, Jr.: Oh, I know Buckingham, yes.

Mr. Buescher: We thought we were out in the sticks, it's pretty much downtown today.

John T. Mason, Jr.: It was quite a journey out to Buckingham, I can tell you.

Mr. Buescher: We went on that bus every night and every morning. No air-conditioning in the buses; it was awfully hot. I had to walk home several nights during the winter. Because of the snow, the bus couldn't get up the hills, but it was okay.

John T. Mason, Jr.: Life in the Washington area was pretty hectic during World War II. I was there.[*] What contacts did you have with Hussey?

Mr. Buescher: Well, you know, I was not high up in the chain then when he was in BuOrd.

John T. Mason, Jr.: You were a quite junior.

Mr. Buescher: Yes, I was a quite junior guy. We made reports to him face to face. We'd go in when there were problems, and he had to know about why things weren't working; we'd explain it to him. When there was a major policy decision we would go down and present the case. I don't remember the budget very much at that time. I was strictly technical, so I'm sure he got involved deeply in the budget.

John T. Mason, Jr.: He did, indeed.

---

[*] The interviewer, Dr. Mason, worked as a civilian in the Office of Naval Intelligence.

Mr. Buescher: But I didn't. Somebody else did that. I was just a technical guy.

John T. Mason, Jr.: But I don't think he had to worry too much with the Congress.

Mr. Buescher: I don't think he had a bit of trouble with Congress.

John T. Mason, Jr.: They came through all right.

Mr. Buescher: Some way or other you had to put something together so they can see it anyhow. But they can't appropriate it to you if you don't give them some numbers.

John T. Mason, Jr.: You were going to say something about Red Schoeffel.

Mr. Buescher: He was the chief of the bureau in the early '50s. There was a big problem in Europe, and they didn't have any work over there. There wasn't enough money, and the U.S. wanted to set up an offshore procurement of ammunition produced by the NATO countries: 20 millimeters and 40 millimeters.*

John T. Mason, Jr.: There was a certain uniformity then in what they used and what we used?

Mr. Buescher: Yes, they could use our ammunition. There was also a political problem. The Communists were coming in and taking advantage of the depression, and the U.S. Government wanted to get some money and work over there.

John T. Mason, Jr.: A very great threat, really, of takeover.

Mr. Buescher: That's right. I went over and set up an offshore procurement program and

---

* NATO—North Atlantic Treaty Organization, which was established in 1949 as a means of coordinating defense against a potential attack from the Soviet Union.

reported back to Schoeffel. That was a real lot of fun.

John T. Mason, Jr.: Where did you set it up?

Mr. Buescher: I went over and stayed in London and worked with the different countries that were going to be involved: Belgium, France, Italy, England. These were the four countries that could get some of the contracts. I worked with them for a while technically, set up the plan for the program. Then I came back to Washington, and we set up a long-term program with on-the-spot inspectors in the plants. We still maintained our control in the BuOrd of the design and things of this sort. We sent these U.S. inspectors as our plant reps to whoever got the contracts over there, and it turned out to be just fine.

John T. Mason, Jr.: It must have been difficult, however, to maintain the kind of management control that you desired when you were manufacturing in foreign plants.

Mr. Buescher: Well, it worked out pretty well. The foreign governments and contractors were told to make the items completely in accordance with our drawings and specifications, and, by gosh, they just followed this 100%. We had these guys on the site who checked on them and made sure everything was going all right. They had their own inspectors too, you see, and they were very conscientious to do it the way we asked them to do it. They did need the business; they needed it badly.

John T. Mason, Jr.: They were contractors, then, for us?

Mr. Buescher: Yes. The Navy Purchasing Office in London was a contracting office, and they let the contracts to all these European contractors.

John T. Mason, Jr.: Did you hear from any of our labor people in this country on this matter?

Mr. Buescher: No.

John T. Mason, Jr.: They went along with it? They weren't being deprived?

Mr. Buescher: We had no problem at that time, not from them as far as I can remember. A number of the U.S. plant reps later came back to the U.S. and were hired into the SP program in different capacities. They were very capable guys, you see.

John T. Mason, Jr.: An old school tie.

Mr. Buescher: Because they had this experience and they were good people. That's what we were looking for.

John T. Mason, Jr.: Well, tell me more about your sojourn in London. How long were you there?

Mr. Buescher: Well, I wasn't there but a few weeks to get it organized and get the contracts out. Then we directed it again from the BuOrd.

John T. Mason, Jr.: That was quite an assignment, wasn't it? You were getting your spurs at this point.

Mr. Buescher: I was really proud of that one, and it worked out so well. BuOrd took over and ran the thing. There was some doubt when I went over as to really what I was going for. Then I got over there, and we organized the program. We got it set up by long conferences with everybody in BuOrd on the telephone, because we were talking to various facets. We're not just talking about my technical people; we're talking about the contractors, the legals, the production people, and everybody else in BuOrd. We brought everybody in and had long conferences over the weekend. It was a lot of fun.

John T. Mason, Jr.: A lot of responsibility.

Mr. Buescher: When I came back, it was all fine, and we knew what we were going to do. We knew what responsibility BuOrd was going to take and how we were going to run it. It worked fine. It was sort of like going into a dark room when I went over there, I'll tell you.

John T. Mason, Jr.: I can see why carrying on a project like that in such a short period of time, you were the logical man to become the chief engineer for SP. You really earned your spurs. Tell me about the immediate postwar period in BuOrd, when the fleet was being cut down and the needs were not nearly as great.

Mr. Buescher: Let me think about that a little bit. As I said before, in my particular case, there was a change in management in the Bureau of Ordnance itself, going from a design group to a technical management group. I came out of the fuze design and technical group, and I came over into a technical management group.

John T. Mason, Jr.: Was this about 1945, 1946?

Mr. Buescher: Yes, I guess it was 1947. We were always very busy. It wasn't like World War I when, I believe, everything dropped out, and there wasn't anything to do. That didn't happen in our case. The production end went down, the size of the maintenance job went down, the number of ships went down, but there was always a new development program, particularly since rockets were becoming more and more the thing and, in particular, aircraft rockets. It was during this period when we worked on development of new rapid-fire guns—5-inch, 3-inch, and 8-inch guns—and later became involved in the guided missile program.

John T. Mason, Jr.: So there were new developments under way?

Mr. Buescher: There were new developments under way, including rockets. There was a new 5-inch high-velocity rocket and a 2.75-inch aircraft rocket. The Sidewinder was a variation of that, which was the heat-seeking one they're using now.* We were quite busy, quite busy.

By the way, Levering Smith was then the technical director of Naval Ordnance Test Station, China Lake and later on the director of the facility.

At this point I got involved with my first standardization program with the U.K.† As a matter of fact, at my SP retirement there was a separate party attended by the British the next day. We had a luncheon at which the U.K. arranged for a farewell for me. I told the group there that I had been involved in projects with the U.K. more years than I had been SP, and I had been in SP for 25 years.

My first project was a 3.75-inch gun ammunition standardization program. This was a shipboard gun, very rapid fire for a 3-inch gun.

John T. Mason, Jr.: Had the British developed something of this sort themselves?

Mr. Buescher: Colonel Probert in the British Army had developed a new type of rifling inside the gun, which was supposed to reduce wear. We took that and built a gun mount all around it. So we were really standardizing on the round of ammunition to go into the guns. Each country would provide the gun mount and handling equipment and develop it. Each country would make its own ammunition or would buy from the other country, since the ammunition was interchangeable in all characteristics.

John T. Mason, Jr.: That's a happy development, isn't it? The interchangeability of weaponry doesn't always exist in NATO.

Mr. Buescher: I think it was firing 90 3-inch rounds a minute. You can imagine the kind of wear that rifle barrel would get. I took on that development and that standardization, and the program lasted six years.

---

* Sidewinder is an air-to-air infrared-homing missile with a speed of approximately Mach 2.5. It has been operational, in various forms, since 1956. It was used extensively in the Vietnam War. For details, see Ron Westrum, Sidewinder: Creative Missile Development at China Lake (Annapolis, Maryland: Naval Institute Press, 1999).
† U.K.—United Kingdom.

John T. Mason, Jr.: I think for the sake of the record you might go into some detail how you organized the standardization effort of that kind. How did you approach it?

Mr. Buescher: It's sort of important in this interview, because it was a forerunner of the way we coordinated some of the things we do in SP. We were standardizing physically on a round of ammunition and how it fit into the gun, the propellant—essentially the characteristics that would impart a very high velocity to the bullet—and the hotness of the propellant was a factor in determining wear in the gun barrel.

John T. Mason, Jr.: Yes.

Mr. Buescher: So we were standardizing those types of things for the ammunition. The equipment that handled the ammunition from the ship's magazine in the bowels of the gun was handled by another part of the bureau and was not standardized with the U.K. We worked very closely to coordinate with them so that all this did fit. We worked closely with the gun barrel people in order to fit, not only physically, but ensure proper performance. We drew up a series of specifications in all the details of what could affect performance, standardized that among ourselves in the U.S., got an agreement, and then we sat down with the U.K. and got their agreement. For example, the ammunition fires by a voltage being applied to a primer in the back of the cartridge case. What we were standardizing would be the voltage, a dimension, a length—things of this sort. So we worked this out in considerable detail and got agreement with the British as to exactly what it would be. Then we were able to each go back and do our own things to develop the ammunition.

John T. Mason, Jr.: What metal was decided upon for the gun barrel?

Mr. Buescher: A molybdenum steel of some sort; I don't remember exactly what it was. Of course, we had technical meetings all the time in liaison with the Brits. We had an organized group that swapped visits, one in the U.K. and a few months later in the U.S. Those visits started in 1949 and went back and forth until late 1955, when the program was completed.

John T. Mason, Jr.: That was about the time the Royal Navy began to decline, too, in 1955.

Mr. Buescher: Yes.

John T. Mason, Jr.: Where was their research located?

Mr. Buescher: We had most of our meetings with their staff in Fort Halsted; that's south of London about 30 miles. They also had some of their technical people in Bath.

John T. Mason, Jr.: Bath, yes.

Mr. Buescher: The reason I mention this is because, as you know, SP is involved in the British Polaris program.

John T. Mason, Jr.: Yes, Bob Wertheim was heavily involved in that.[*]

Mr. Buescher: Yes. That was my first project with the U.K., and that worked out fine.

John T. Mason, Jr.: You were talking about the fact that your work continued at a high level, although the Navy as such was being diminished in size.

Mr. Buescher: We were pinching pennies, but we were getting the job done—both the rocket ammunition and gun ammunition. We also had the explosive ordnance disposal; we had pyrotechnics in our group; we had a lot of things of this sort. All this was very active.

John T. Mason, Jr.: Say something more about the disposal aspect.

---

[*] Commander Robert H. Wertheim, USN. The oral history of Wertheim, who retired as a rear admiral, is in the Naval Institute collection.

Mr. Buescher: We had one group of guys in my branch, under me, that worked with the ordnance explosive group in Indian Head to design and develop all these gadgets used for disposal. Maybe it was a limpet for putting on the side of a ship or maybe a land mine or any kind of thing that they needed for use against the enemy or for blowing up our own ammunition that needed to be disposed of. There wasn't a lot of money in that, but a lot of fun in it. There were many strange gadgets in those days, such as a one-time-use thing, but it was interesting.

John T. Mason, Jr.: There were this type of thing dreamed up by the President himself and Churchill.* Strange gadgets weren't they?

Mr. Buescher: That's quite right.

John T. Mason, Jr.: And they had to be disposed of.

Mr. Buescher: That's right.

John T. Mason, Jr.: Was there any constraint placed upon you by the Congress in this area? Was there any pressure to destroy ammunition?

Mr. Buescher: No. It was only ammunition you didn't know what else to do with it. We weren't destroying our ammunition, say, as a disarmament. It may be a bomb dropped, or maybe something happened to something aboard a ship or on land, and you had to get rid of it. It may be that in World War II it was enemy stuff more than our own. Later on, during peacetime, there was a lot of our new ordnance. However, they'd come in and anything we developed, they'd want to know how to defeat it, not tactically but it's lying there, you see, what to do with the things to dispose of it. So they came up with all kinds of gadgets.

---

* Franklin D. Roosevelt was President of the United States from March 1933 to April 1945. Winston S. Churchill was Prime Minister of the United Kingdom from 1940 to 1945.

John T. Mason, Jr.: You mentioned earlier the Sidewinder as a development out at China Lake. What involvement did you have in that? What is the date time for that? That was the early '50s, wasn't it?

Mr. Buescher: Yes, the early '50s.

John T. Mason, Jr.: Freddie Withington was there then, in the bureau.*

Mr. Buescher: Fred Withington. I couldn't remember Freddie's name a while ago. There are a couple more whose names I haven't thought of. NOTS was the development activity, and we were the management bureau. Later on, we gave them the money, we set up the specifications and worked with them on this development. Then we put it in production in the bureau and bought it. When we produced the thing, we procured it from the bureau. The same way with the 2.75-inch rocket. I think we've almost gotten up to the Korean War.

John T. Mason, Jr.: Withington considered the Sidewinder the greatest achievement of his time there.

Mr. Buescher: A very valuable thing, very valuable.

John T. Mason, Jr.: And continues to be.

Mr. Buescher: And continues to be, that's right. It sort of rules out any real effectiveness of close-in fighting of aircraft. You know you're going to get it if you come near one of those things; it goes right up your tailpipe.

John T. Mason, Jr.: Were there any other bits of ordnance, pieces of ordnance, developed

---

* Rear Admiral Frederic S. Withington, USN, served as Chief of the Bureau of Ordnance from 1954 to 1958. His oral history is in the Naval Institute collection.

John B. Buescher, Interview #1 (11/17/81) – Page 32

in that period that continue to be effective as weaponry?

Mr. Buescher: I can't tell you because I'm too far away from it. I'd been in SP 25 years, and I don't know whether or not some of these things are still in use.

John T. Mason, Jr.: You did mention off tape the ASROC and Weapon A.*

Mr. Buescher: Yes. I suspect that they are simply because I don't recall hearing about a lot of these things being replaced, 5-inch high-velocity rockets and bombardment rockets from aircraft, shooting against ships and things of this sort. After I left the bureau, which was BuWeps when I left it, not much money was put in the type of thing I had been working on. Guided missiles, Terrier and Talos, came along.† We were completely involved in that. It was our responsibility to develop—starting at the front—the fuzes, the warheads, explosive, the rocket motors—

John T. Mason, Jr.: For the three T's?‡

Mr. Buescher: Yes. That was our responsibility and we used Allegheny Ballistic Laboratory to develop and produce rocket propulsion motors. To some extent the Naval Test Station in Indian Head were involved.

John T. Mason, Jr.: You had the same operational control on their development, did you?

Mr. Buescher: Yes, my branch did.

---

* ASROC—antisubmarine rocket. It entered the fleet in the early 1960s in new-construction ships and in FRAM I destroyer conversions. Weapon A, known at different times as Weapon Able and Weapon Alfa, was a trainable launcher that fired antisubmarine rockets that contained explosive charges. The range was 400-800 yards. Weapon A entered the fleet in the early 1950s
† The Terrier, a radar-beam-riding surface-to-air missile began in the late 1940s as an outgrowth of the Talos supersonic test vehicle. Its first shipboard launch was in 1951. Operational testing on board the Mississippi began in July 1954. The missile first went into fleet use on board the cruiser Boston (CAG-1), which was recommissioned on 1 November 1955 after conversion to a guided missile ship.
‡ The other "T" in the antiair guided missile family was Tartar.

John B. Buescher, Interview #1 (11/17/81) – Page 33

John T. Mason, Jr.: And yet I recall that when the missile system became operational in the fleet, they were unsatisfactory, and that's when Eli Reich was put on the project.* Why was that?

Mr. Buescher: They had taken an experimental design and put it into production. The design agency was the Applied Physics Lab, and I don't mean to be critical of APL when I say this. They are research and development. They know very little about production or production engineering. The missile system, particularly the electronics, was not engineered for production. Those controls and configuration controls and everything else that you need to do—those necessary management disciplines did not exist. The missiles themselves were experimental things rather than made for production and produced by production means.

John T. Mason, Jr.: They were experimental prototypes, then?

Mr. Buescher: That's right. That's what it was. They went into production, and then they had to stop and turn around and start all over again, if you remember, simply because of this problem. It was the first missile the Navy had been involved in and the first thing they had produced in quantity of this sort. That was the problem.

John T. Mason, Jr.: I recall Eli was sort of a little SP project unto himself with great power in that area. Did you take part in any of the testing projects out in the Pacific or the islands?

Mr. Buescher: No. I was not involved in that. We supplied material but were not involved in the formulation or the conduct of the tests.

John T. Mason, Jr.: Were you involved in Mustin's Argus operation in the South

---

* This problem is covered in the Naval Institute oral history of Rear Admiral Eli T. Reich, USN (Ret.).

Atlantic?*

Mr. Buescher: From the same standpoint. I know Wertheim was aboard some of these ships, and he was involved in some of the firings, but our group was not.

John T. Mason, Jr.: Willis Lee came along toward the end of World War II, came back from the fleet and set up what became OpTEvFor.† Was this something the bureau contributed to?

Mr. Buescher: I don't know about the bureau, but my branch was not involved in the formulation of the OpTEvFor, but we did send things for the evaluation. There was probably some group, particularly the chief of the bureau, that was involved in setting that thing up with the fleet. But it did need someplace to go to test and evaluate equipments under tactical conditions.

John T. Mason, Jr.: A very happy idea.

Mr. Buescher: It is. I say that, yet you'll find that SP did not use OpTEvFor. That doesn't make any difference. It was a good idea and is a very useful situation. You need it. SP acted as its own evaluator.

John T. Mason, Jr.: It tied the operational aspect more closely to the development of weaponry. You mentioned Dahlgren once. Did you have more to do with Dahlgren than ordnance?

Mr. Buescher: Dahlgren, Indian Head, and Naval Ordnance Test Station in China Lake

---

* Project Argus, a high-altitude test of nuclear weapons, was conducted in 1958 by Task Force 88, under the command of Rear Admiral Lloyd M. Mustin, USN. The oral history of Mustin, who retired as a vice admiral, is in the Naval Institute collection.
† In the summer of 1945 Vice Admiral Willis A. Lee, Jr., USN, commanded Task Force 69, which conducted anti-kamikaze operational tests in Casco Bay, Maine. The force evolved into the Operational Development Force and was later renamed Operational Test and Evaluation Force (OpTEvFor).

were really our development test activities.* If a gun, like a 3-inch/50, was mounted aboard ship and there was going to be a tactical test by OpTEvFor of the system, we were involved because we furnished the ammunition for that. They reported back any deficiencies of performance. But VT fuze testing, all that kind of thing was done at Dahlgren against aircraft or other targets. We used New Mexico School of Mines in a limited capacity, and a bunch of other small activities were involved. They all got involved in a limited capacity, but the test ranges were these people, and we did use OpTEvFor for special jobs.

John T. Mason, Jr.: Going back to the early part of World War II, when we got the right to manufacture the Bofors gun and the Oerlikon, the bureau was involved in that.†

Mr. Buescher: We had to convert those designs over to standard measurement rather than metric, and we had to do what we had to do to make them useable in this country, so there were slight changes, but dimensionally the requirements were not radically changed.

John T. Mason, Jr.: We just took over the manufacture of those guns, didn't we?

Mr. Buescher: That's right. We did our drawings; that was the main thing. We couldn't talk to our U.S. contractors in metrics. They were not set up to handle metrics, and we had had little experience with metrics.

John T. Mason, Jr.: And then there was compensation to the Swedes and the Swiss, weren't there, for the use of their designs?

Mr. Buescher: Yes. I guess they were paid money. I don't know how much. That way, I would think, about 1942 we got involved in that program. During the war we also were

---

* The name China Lake is often associated with the Naval Ordnance Test Station, Inyokern, California.
† In the early 1940s the Navy's Bureau of Ordnance obtained licenses for U.S. manufacture of two foreign-designed light antiaircraft guns, the Swiss 20-millimeter Oerlikon and the Swedish 40-millimeter Bofors. They were mainstays on U.S. Navy ships throughout World War II and beyond.

involved to make some ammunition for the French battleship, the Richelieu.* We took their drawings and converted them over and went out and bought ammunition for this use.

John T. Mason, Jr.: And she was in Dakar and we brought her over to New York, didn't we?

Mr. Buescher: Yes. That was real interesting, too, you know. We worked with the Free French some on that.

John T. Mason, Jr.: The other French were too reluctant.†

Mr. Buescher: Exactly right.

John T. Mason, Jr.: Oh, you might say something since you did mention the metric system the more recent attempt to inflict that upon us in this country. You must have ideas on the subject.

Mr. Buescher: Yes, I've got my own ideas. The U.S. is not ready for metric. They've got a long way to go to get ready for it. Nobody's doing really a lot to get ready for it.

John T. Mason, Jr.: How do you get ready for it?

Mr. Buescher: Well, you get ready by starting to use it more and more, and we feel there's a certain outlay of money's got to take place. We found it very difficult in SP programs to do it because all of our systems—each generation of our equipment—the Polaris A-1, A-2, A-3, C-3, Trident, C-4.* These systems are all evolutionary, you see, in that we're building on what we've done before. All the complete weapon systems never change, only parts of

---

* The 35,000-ton French battleship Richelieu was completed at Brest in early 1940. When France collapsed in the spring of 1940, the ship was ordered to Dakar, French West Africa, where she was subjected to British attacks. In 1943, following Allied landings in Northwest Africa, the ship was sent to the New York Navy Yard for repairs and rearming. After that was completed, she operated as part of the Royal Navy.
† France was occupied by German forces from the spring of 1940 onward. Free French forces existed in exile and in resistance movements.

them.

For instance, when the C-4 Trident I came along, the weapons system, we found that the new ship was under design using U.S. standard inch measurements. We interfaced with the ship in many places. I don't believe NavSea is going to change to metrics for a long time. We would find its system and the interface between the weapon system and another system, very difficult. We may have done it in the missile only, as compared to the rest of the things that SP had furnished—fire control, navigation, launcher. But still, there would have been a difficulty in interfacing between those ship-installed equipments and the missile. U.S. industry is not really geared up yet to go metric.

When we started Trident C-4 the issue came up. The missile people pushed very hard to give a go to metrics and because we had parts of the system that were never going to be changed for the Trident, I wrote up a policy thing. Levering Smith signed it out, saying that we were not going to change to metrics.[†] I suspect that will continue.

When the D-5 came along, that's the next system, you have the same situation and it makes it very difficult to work out interfaces and things of this sort, and in a double system of that sort. You either ought to change or not change. Whoever is the first large program to go metrics will need to be prepared to do a lot of pioneering in this field and be prepared to fund it.

John T. Mason, Jr.: You used that as an illustration, and it's true across the board, I suppose, in industry.

Mr. Buescher: In the MX system, a new weapon system, the Air Force had an opportunity.[‡] It wasn't evolutionary. Everything was brand new, but when they got down to it and found out what it was going to cost and they were having so much trouble with the budget, as you know, they cut it out. They went back to the standard measurement system. They had it in their plan to go to metric all the way, but it just cost too much.

---

[*] The Trident submarine-launched ballistic missile entered the fleet in the late 1970s.
[†] Rear Admiral Levering Smith, USN, served as director of the Special Projects Office/Strategic Systems Projects Office from 16 February 1965 to 14 November 1977.
[‡] The Air Force's MX Peacekeeper is a four-stage intercontinental ballistic missile designed to deliver ten re-entry vehicles at ranges of about 6,000 miles. Peacekeeper made its first flight in 1983 and achieved initial operational capability in 1986 when the first ten went on alert.

When they started cutting things out, it just went.

John T. Mason, Jr.: We have arrived at the outbreak of the Korean War, which came as a great surprise and left the Navy in a bad position because Secretary Johnson had cut down so drastically on funds for anything and everything.*

Mr. Buescher: The Korean War didn't create any real surge of development activity, because it was always thought of as a short-term thing.

John T. Mason, Jr.: It didn't seem like much of a war at the beginning, did it?

Mr. Buescher: It was generally thought to be a short-term engagement.

John T. Mason, Jr.: And we always feared getting involved on the continent of Asia.

Mr. Buescher: That's right. The weapons that were in existence in the fleet were considered satisfactory for this short-term thing. However, there was a breakthrough by the Koreans, tanks through the American lines, the Allied lines, bringing tanks south. There needed to be some way to combat these large tanks. The Bureau of Ordnance gave NOTS requirements to develop a rocket fired from an aircraft, a shaped-charge rocket, to defeat the tanks.

John T. Mason, Jr.: It must have been a rush order, was it?

Mr. Buescher: Very rush order, very high priority. At the same time, two of us engineers in the Bureau of Ordnance separately undertook a parallel development using the gun factory for purposes of the rocket fabrication.

John T. Mason, Jr.: Was this in response to this rush order?

---

* Louis A. Johnson served as Secretary of Defense from 28 March 1949 to 19 September 1950.

Mr. Buescher: Yes. We in the bureau weren't really given the job. We just undertook it because we thought we had some ideas too.

John T. Mason, Jr.: Was there another project being developed simultaneously?

Mr. Buescher: Yes, at NOTS. NOTS ended up on a very rush scale by developing a new six-and-a-half-inch rocket with a shaped charge head and an electric fuze. The rocket was fired from the aircraft. The rocket was tried in the battlefield in Korea, and it was very effective against the Korean tanks. At the same time, we in the bureau developed ours and used Dahlgren for testing. We used standard components except for the rocket head—a standard fuze, standard motor, and everything. This was very effective too. We got very deep penetration of heavy plate at Dahlgren, went right through it. Because it used a mechanical fuze and had standard components out of the 5-inch rocket already stocked in quantity by the Navy and we didn't have a problem with an electric fuze—with battery life and things of this sort, as did the NOTS rocket—our rocket superseded the NOTS development and was produced in large quantities by BuOrd.

John T. Mason, Jr.: I take it you two had set aside anything you were doing and concentrated completely on this project.

Mr. Buescher: That's about it.

John T. Mason, Jr.: But then what about the manufacturing?

Mr. Buescher: There was a small order of the NOTS type put into production, a couple of thousand, and then main production went in on the one we developed. NOTS got there first by about a month, but in the long run they had bought hundreds of thousands of ours. We felt real good about that, because we had very limited resources, and we got this whole thing into in production and tactical use.

John T. Mason, Jr.: You had some fertile ideas.

Mr. Buescher: Yes, I believe so.

John T. Mason, Jr.: What company manufactured them for you?

Mr. Buescher: The bureau went out to about six or eight different contractors to buy quantities.

John T. Mason, Jr.: You mean component parts or the whole thing?

Mr. Buescher: They had millions of fuzes in stock, you see. And the rocket motors, they had them in stock. It was just a matter of buying the rocket head and loading it with explosive. So they went out and bought these metal parts from six or eight different contractors, and I don't know who they were. Maybe they were buying half a million each, rocket heads, and we used NAD, Crane, for loading with explosives.[*] So it worked out very well. We were real proud of that.

John T. Mason, Jr.: What was the time element involved in your development of it and the manufacturing and getting it out to Korea?

Mr. Buescher: I suspect we took about three or four months for development and then almost immediately went into production. I've kind of lost track of those numbers, but I think it was

John T. Mason, Jr.: And meanwhile the enemy was advancing.

Mr. Buescher: The enemy had been stopped in the meantime. The Navy's new rocket helped, among a lot of other things. But the Navy did have an aircraft rocket. They could send a plane off of a carrier and knock out a tank that was coming along, which they didn't have before.

---

[*] NAD—Naval Ammunition Depot, Crane, Indiana.

John T. Mason, Jr.: What about the Inchon invasion?* Was BuOrd involved in any way?

Mr. Buescher: As far as I know, BuOrd was not involved other than furnishing standard ammunition for bombardment, as I recall, and for air support.

John T. Mason, Jr.: You implied, I take it, that we had an ample supply of ammunition on hand at the outbreak of the Korean War?

Mr. Buescher: That's right. Enough that didn't require a crash production program. I suspect some procurements were made.

John T. Mason, Jr.: How did this happen, because there had been a stale period in there when—

Mr. Buescher: There was an awful lot bought during World War II which was in storage, you see. Instead of just throwing that stuff away, they didn't stop the production lines on V-E Day or V-J Day; they had to sort of cut them off and all of this was in the pipeline then.† So they'd store it, that's all. You have to have a certain quantity for war readiness, quantities ready to go.

John T. Mason, Jr.: Isn't there also the element of deterioration, though, in storage?

Mr. Buescher: There is. Not all components go, but those that are chemicals, for instance, propellants and things of this sort. You can keep them around for a long time, you know, 15, 20, 30 years. We've had Polaris A-1s in being in the fleet 20 years between us and the Brits, you see. And Polaris is a rather sophisticated type of thing. In BuOrd we were using rather simple propellants and simple explosives, which last one heck of a long time.

---

* On 15 September 1950, U.S. troops under the command of General of the Army Douglas MacArthur made an amphibious landing at Inchon, the port for Seoul, South Korea. The surprise landing, 150 miles behind enemy lines, temporarily turned the tide of war in favor of United Nations forces.
† V-E Day and V-J Day marked the Allied victories in Europe and Japan in 1945.

John T. Mason, Jr.: I know in the case of mines, when we're using World War I types.

Mr. Buescher: That's right.

John T. Mason, Jr.: You felt that that was your contribution.

Mr. Buescher: That was our contribution. There were other things, but this was the major contribution and the fact that there were some explosives; there were some limpet mines.

John T. Mason, Jr.: There must have been concern related to the dangers of the mining operations in Korean waters. It was rather extensive in one area in Pusan and that part of the peninsula. This didn't come to your project?

Mr. Buescher: There were BuOrd efforts but not involving me.

John T. Mason, Jr.: You might go on and tell me about your other activities in the bureau in the early '50s before you ever came to SP. What occupied your attention at that time?

Mr. Buescher: As I mentioned before, it was during this period that we worked on the aircraft rocket, the 3-inch/70 guns, high-velocity 8-inch guns, both of them rapid-fire guns, and the guided missiles development. I think we've touched on all of these.

John T. Mason, Jr.: You might pause and tell me something about your family. You say you have two children.

Mr. Buescher: I have two children. My son John was born in 1950; he's married and lives here locally.

John T. Mason, Jr.: What is his occupation?

Mr. Buescher: At the present time he's in the throes of defending his thesis for a doctorate.

John T. Mason, Jr.: In what subject?

Mr. Buescher: Oriental religions.

John T. Mason, Jr.: Oriental religions. How amazing. How did he select that?

Mr. Buescher: He got involved with that at the University of Virginia, and the first week of December he goes down. He's been about three years getting this last phase of writing the thesis and getting all that done,

John T. Mason, Jr.: It's quite a process.

Mr. Buescher: It's quite a process. It's all been around his neck. Even when he went to Japan for a year to work, he was still working on it over there. He stopped by India on the way back, and he's been after it ever since.

John T. Mason, Jr.: Did he master Japanese as a language?

Mr. Buescher: He can speak it. A very funny thing happened over there. They studied it a little bit, not much, before they went, and he's very good at languages.

John T. Mason, Jr.: Is his wife also?

Mr. Buescher: She's pretty good too. They were both speaking. They taught English, completely in English, but they got so they could talk pretty well with the people over there. He said that something about the Japanese has difficulty in accepting the fact that a foreigner such as he can speak Japanese.

John T. Mason, Jr.: Never, never.

Mr. Buescher: No. They never accept that, you see. And he said he'd call a store up on the phone and talk to the clerk to see if they had something. They would locate it, and he would make an appointment to go by to pick it up. He'd go over there and walk in talking Japanese, and they couldn't understand a word he said.

John T. Mason, Jr.: But they accepted it on the telephone; it was business.

Mr. Buescher: Everything was fine on the telephone when they couldn't see him.

John T. Mason, Jr.: And what does he intend to do with his doctorate then?

Mr. Buescher: I think he's intending to teach college.

John T. Mason, Jr.: Well, that's a very limited field. There aren't many people in that field.

Mr. Buescher: That's right.

John T. Mason, Jr.: Does he have any connections? Does the University of Virginia have an Oriental section?

Mr. Buescher: Yes, yes. They have an Oriental section. There are a number of places across the United States that have had this. This is in connection with Asian studies, University of Wisconsin, a couple of places in Canada, Harvard, I don't know. Four or five places; I don't know where they are.

John T. Mason, Jr.: They have one child?

Mr. Buescher: No. My daughter has the child; my granddaughter is 15. My daughter lives in Los Angeles.* She's married and divorced.

John T. Mason, Jr.: Is she a professional? Does she work?

Mr. Buescher: She finished Syracuse in art, commercial design, and that's what she does for a living.

John T. Mason, Jr.: That's very lucrative.

Mr. Buescher: Yes. She loves it, she really loves it. She ran a business here in Washington for a number of years, four or five years. She was born in 1944, so that makes her a little bit older than John. My granddaughter at the present time is in India going to school.

John T. Mason, Jr.: India?

Mr. Buescher: India, of all places. We've got a family, but they're sort of spread out.

---

* Mr. Buescher's daughter, Siri Gian Khalsa, now lives in Falls Church, Virginia.

Interview Number 2 with Mr. John B. Buescher

Place: Mr. Buescher's residence in Falls Church, Virginia

Date: Thursday, 28 January 1982

Interviewer: John T. Mason, Jr.

John T. Mason, Jr.: John, I'm delighted to see you today in the wintertime. You certainly have a winter scene here. Last time when we broke off, I think you had completed your remarks about your operations during the Korean War; you were still in BuOrd. Do you want to take up the story? What did you turn your attention to after that?

Mr. Buescher: During that period, BuOrd and BuAer and BuShips and the Navy material bureaus went through reorganization.* All of my duties changed, and I got into other things such as bombs, rockets, and warheads—parts that I had not been in before.

John T. Mason, Jr.: That must have been a welcome change.

Mr. Buescher: It was a welcome change, but I wasn't with it long enough to really get too deep into it. Then I had the offer to go to SP and I left and went to SP.

John T. Mason, Jr.: Did you accomplish anything specific in BuOrd or BuWeps after the Korean enterprise?

Mr. Buescher: It was just a continuation of what we were doing during the Korean War. I set out to try to better organize the warhead program in the new area I had taken over, but I just wasn't there long enough. I got it somewhat better organized.

John T. Mason, Jr.: What were your ideas?

---

* Effective 1 December 1959, the Bureau of Aeronautics was merged with the Bureau of Ordnance. The new organization was known as the Bureau of Naval Weapons. The first chief of the combined bureau was Rear Admiral Paul D. Stroop, USN. His oral history is in the Naval Institute collection.

Mr. Buescher: They had too many people running in all directions, doing their own thing rather than trying to do it as a cohesive group, and that's what I was trying to overcome. I got into a lot of battles with various activities, and I was trying to make them work together.

John T. Mason, Jr.: It was project management?

Mr. Buescher: Project management, and although we were developing new bombs and new rockets and things of this sort, it wasn't getting there, simply because it needed to be pulled together. So I spent maybe a year on that, and that's when I left and went to SP.

John T. Mason, Jr.: That was good training for what you jumped into in SP, was it not?

Mr. Buescher: It was good training. The whole bit I had been in in BuOrd and BuWeps was good training, because the ammunition is somewhat different from other things such as fire control. It was held differently for many reasons; one of them is that these are things that you make in quantity. You had to have a discipline about how you go about doing your business if you want the same quality of material to come out and be produced from lot to lot over the years. That's what we were doing. We were turning them out in such large, large quantities that you had to have the discipline in order to control it. So all that background was really—

John T. Mason, Jr.: And that's something that experience teaches you, isn't it?

Mr. Buescher: Yes, you learn it the hard way, I think.

John T. Mason, Jr.: Not out of a textbook.

Mr. Buescher: No. That's the big experience that I took over in SP and I applied in SP, and I'll tell you about that as we get into it.

John T. Mason, Jr.: Yes, yes indeed. And this was your baby; you saw the need for it there in BuWeps.

Mr. Buescher: That's right.

John T. Mason, Jr.: Did you get the cooperation of the director?

Mr. Buescher: I had no problem there, no problem with the director.

John T. Mason, Jr.: With the personnel?

Mr. Buescher: People who had been involved in this program for many years were doing things their own way, and I was trying to whip them into line. And we were getting there. A lot of blood was shed.

John T. Mason, Jr.: Did it continue after you left? Did it develop as you had envisioned?

Mr. Buescher: It did improve the program. My idea was to take some of these people who really hadn't produced and fire them out of the program. I wanted to get them out of the program and give the jobs to those guys who were willing to sit down and do the job right. I hadn't reached that point but almost. I don't want to go into the names of the people in conversation.

John T. Mason, Jr.: Most of those people were civil servants, were they?

Mr. Buescher: Some of them were civil servants, some of them were people from universities, some of them were contractors. So it was just a mix of them all. It wasn't necessarily the staff in BuWeps; it was the contributing organization that I was having trouble with. They weren't speaking to each other; they were fighting that it ought to be their idea that is accepted. You can't get a job done that way.

John T. Mason, Jr.: Whatever job it is, it's teamwork.

Mr. Buescher: It's teamwork, and we didn't have it. We were getting there.

John T. Mason, Jr.: Is this what called the attention of the people in SP to you?

Mr. Buescher: I don't know. I had been very active in many of the BuOrd programs, including guided missiles and rockets. I had taken the lead in this ammunition area over the years in establishing program management.

For instance, the R&D community had always been hamstrung for money. I'll give you an example. Under the law, the money appropriated by Congress, we didn't have to use RDT-80 money. Once we got a design and wanted to go out and buy quantities and start testing, we could go into production funds. Very few people knew that I was able to break that barrier and get a lot of money to support the program as a result. We had a lot more money than anybody else in BuWeps did. It took more money because we bought more things. We had to test more things because it was destructive testing. I know the gun mount people and the gun people always shook their heads and said, "Where did we get all that money?" It was relatively small in today's terms, but in comparison with the rest of the organization, we had a lot more money. We were getting the production money. I got that whole thing approved as a way of doing business.

John T. Mason, Jr.: How could that have been not observed by other people there who would realize that this was the avenue to take?

Mr. Buescher: They were always working off of R&D models. We weren't. We were pushing to get a final model of a bullet or rocket or missile or a component thereof and to make them in a quantity that we knew we could produce. What were we getting out of the R&D program? All we were getting out of it was a set of drawings. You test them the best you can and sometimes they work; you don't know why. And sometimes they don't work, and you work your head off to find why. But often you end up with a set of drawings representing an item, and you don't really know why that worked but it works.

You don't fully understand it all. So what you're trying to do is fix that design, get a good set of documentation, and then produce it to that documentation. You control the changes to it and set up an inspection program so you know what you've got. If there are any variances, you know what the variances are, and you know on what piece and in what article.

John T. Mason, Jr.: So it's that control that really is the key to the thing.

Mr. Buescher: In the BuOrd and BuWeps makeup there was an R&D group, there was a production group, there was a quality control group. You can't turn over the design to a production group, as so often happens, and just say, "I've done my job as an R&D man. Here, you take these drawings and go out and buy it." You've got to maintain control of that design. You've got to hold on to it. You have got to insist that they make it just the way you tell them to. Any time they want to make changes to make it more producible, to make it cheaper, or for other reasons, it's all got to come back to you. If you don't, you don't have control, you see.

And you've got to watch that inspection very carefully. BuOrd had a good inspection group headed up by Captain Ben Lubelsky over the years. They really had developed the whole concept of quality control for mass-produced items, and they concentrated in our area, in ammunition and explosives. But we had to tell them what it was we wanted inspected. We had to tell them in detail, dimension by dimension. We had to tell them the importance of any variance from those dimensions. And when there was a variance, they had to come back to us, and we'd say if we could accept that or not accept it. So this is all part of the discipline I'm talking about that I was involved in and helped to develop in the BuOrd and BuWeps period, you see.

John T. Mason, Jr.: You and Eli Reich must have conferred, because this is the approach he made to the 3-T problem, isn't it?

Mr. Buescher: It's the same as 3-T. The torpedo program had a hell of a problem, a hell of a problem. Eli worked awfully hard in that to try to get the torpedo business back in line, and it was from this standpoint, you see, configuration control and so on. He may have told you about it.

John T. Mason, Jr.: Yes, he did.

Mr. Buescher: Eli and I didn't work together, because he was in one program, and I was in the other program.

John T. Mason, Jr.: But you had like philosophies.

Mr. Buescher: We had our hands full. That's the reason I never got into Eli's area.

John T. Mason, Jr.: I would think you did have your hands full in trying to impose a system like that upon a disparate group.

Mr. Buescher: It worked. It worked.

John T. Mason, Jr.: It seems to me that this was an idea whose time had arrived. It had not been in practice before, had it?

Mr. Buescher: Not really. And they had never really produced things in the same quantities that we did in World War II and the Korean War.

John T. Mason, Jr.: Was it used in the program with the contact fuzes?

Mr. Buescher: Oh, yes. The contact fuze, the VT fuzes, the bomb fuze—all that was in our area.

John T. Mason, Jr.: And, of course, they went back to World War II.

Mr. Buescher: Yes. It was something that evolved really during that period that is still coming along, and SP needed it, I'll tell you.

John T. Mason, Jr.: Yes, I guess it did.

Mr. Buescher: As for how I got in SP, I'm not quite sure how that all came about, but I have suspected that the chief engineer of BuOrd, Mr. Girard, and Albert Wertheimer, who was an old-timer in there and who I had worked with, may have had something to do with it. Of course, I knew Levering; I knew Admiral Raborn from his duty on BuOrd, and I knew Captain Colwell from the deputy director of SP.[*] I knew the chief engineer—that's the chief engineer in SP at the time who left and went to BuOrd as chief engineer. I had worked with all of these people when they were in BuOrd.

John T. Mason, Jr.: He left SP?

Mr. Buescher: Yes. At about the time the decision was made to go away from the Jupiter missile to go to a solid propellant, he got the offer to be chief engineer of BuOrd. He's an old BuOrd man and he took that job, and I knew him real well and respected him.

John T. Mason, Jr.: That happened around December of 1955?

Mr. Buescher: Now, it was about October of 1956 when the Navy really authorized this thing. Nineteen fifty-five is when—

John T. Mason, Jr.: When Raborn came.

Mr. Buescher: Yes, that's when they took on the job with the Jupiter missile. But it was about a year later—I think it was October of 1956, I'm not sure—that authorization was

---

[*] Rear Admiral William F. Raborn, Jr., USN, was director of the Special Projects Office, which developed the Polaris submarine-launched ballistic missile system. He held the post from 1955 to 1962, being promoted to vice admiral in 1960. His Polaris oral history is in the Naval Institute collection. Captain John B. Colwell, USN, served as deputy director of the Fleet Ballistic Missile Project from 1955 to 1958. The oral history of Colwell, who retired as vice admiral, is in the Naval Institute collection.

given for the Navy to come up with a proposal for a solid-propellant missile. I guess you know all the reasons for getting away from the liquids.

John T. Mason, Jr.: Yes.

Mr. Buescher: We don't need to go into all that. I was involved in that. I was branch engineer in the RE-2 organization, the BuOrd organization, and we helped SP come up with that proposal. We brought up a propellant expert, and all of us got involved in this thing so that the Navy could make a decision, the Navy and DoD.* So I had a little background in SP, in the program, before I went over there, not much.

John T. Mason, Jr.: You weren't a perfect stranger to this.

Mr. Buescher: No, I wasn't a perfect stranger, and I wasn't a perfect stranger to a number of the people that had gone over there. When I got to SP—

John T. Mason, Jr.: This was the first of January?

Mr. Buescher: Yes. I got sick and went to the hospital and I was out about a month.

John T. Mason, Jr.: This is in 1957 when you were out?

Mr. Buescher: It was in November of 1956. I essentially went from the hospital to the new job in SP. I had my appendix removed,

John T. Mason, Jr.: Getting ready for the new job.

Mr. Buescher: I guess I was, yes. So when I went over to SP, I had a PD that said "advisor to the director and chief advisor to the director."† Before I got there, SP started

---

* DoD—Department of Defense.
† PD—position description.

out that there were just four or five people. Everybody was on the staff of Admiral Raborn, and as time went on it began to be a working organization. It was not really, but they were trying to get this Jupiter thing squared away, and they began to reorganize and regroup.

The physical location of that chief engineer's job had been placed on the technical director's staff but still advisor to the technical director and the director. That was the place for it; they had done it right. I say this because in an organization of that sort, people with so many backgrounds and so many ways of doing things and working together, they were very suspicious of anybody outside the direct chain of command. Had I been on Raborn's staff—had that job been placed on Raborn's staff and worked there, he would have always been an outsider to the technical division. So the job was where it should have been, and it worked fine.

John T. Mason, Jr.: And the technical director, who was he?

Mr. Buescher: It was Captain Grayson Merrill first and then Levering Smith.[*] It was soon after I got there that Levering Smith came up. For instance, while Merrill was preparing to leave, Levering was the deputy, and then he took over.

John T. Mason, Jr.: Was J. B. Colwell there then?

Mr. Buescher: J. B. was there, yes. I enjoyed working with J. B. He was a real gentleman, a real fine guy. Here I was with just a general job sheet, and believe it or not, nobody ever told me what to do after that. That was it, you see. You go in and find what you can do best and apply whatever your skills are and go ahead.

John T. Mason, Jr.: Carte blanche?

Mr. Buescher: I stayed that way the whole time, 25 years. Anywhere I felt I ought to be or

---

[*] Captain Grayson Merrill, USN, was technical director of the Polaris program until his retirement from active duty in 1957. His oral history is in the Naval Institute collection.

anything I wanted to get into—even if it was just personnel management and didn't relate to me or technical business—if I wanted to get into it, I got involved and nobody ever said anything.

John T. Mason, Jr.: That system is predicated upon having a man who has the talent, to give him free rein.

Mr. Buescher: There had been sort of a reorganization in which SP had established branches. I think that's the next thing I should tell you about in SP. In SP 22 there was a captain whose background was BuShips; in SP 23 we had electronics, Captain Harold; in SP 24 we had another captain from BuShips in navigation; in SP 25 we had another captain who I think had been in the White Sands Testing Group; in SP 26 we had another BuShips captain; and in SP 27 we had a captain from the old BuOrd missile group. Then we had sub-groups—sections—in the missile group. One of the sections was the front end and warhead, where Bob Wertheim was, you see.

That's a strange organization. How they arrived at these people, I don't know. Some of them were very talented, some of them not so talented, and some of them didn't know how to work with the group.

John T. Mason, Jr.: Some of them were famous already

Mr. Buescher: No, not really famous.

John T. Mason, Jr.: Wasn't Dr. Draper head of one of the groups?

Mr. Buescher: Dr. Draper headed up the Draper Labs, which came under SP 23 cog for the development of guidance.[*] Draper was not in SP. We were in the process of selecting sub-system contractors to go with each of these branches.

First, let me tell you about the people. What this was was really an ordnance

---

[*] Dr. Stark Draper of the Massachusetts Institute of Technology had an important role in the development of the inertial navigation systems used in Polaris missiles and later in the space missions sent to the moon.

program headed up by all these people with completely different philosophies on how to get a job done. How NavSea—BuShips then—could get the job done and how the ordnance community gets it done are entirely and completely different. Building ships is far different from building an intricate weapons system. I think that the first thing I found is that they had a lot of people, very energetic, very dedicated, running around trying to do their own thing again, and very few people in the position to pull them together as a team. They weren't a team. They were a bunch of fighting tigers. I think that, again, is where I felt I should concentrate. We had wonderful talent. We had anybody anywhere we wanted to go, and SP could pull on people, industry, government labs. Anywhere in the government-industrial complex we could pull on people for their services.

John T. Mason, Jr.: Raborn told me about that letter he carried in his pocket.

Mr. Buescher: That's right. So we didn't really need, as chief engineer, a guy running around telling all these experts in their field how to do their job. But we did need something to pull these people together and let them work as a team. Levering was very talented. If there was a technical question, he had the expertise, and I would advise him. And then he would, in his way, make the decision to settle these kinds of problems.

For instance, I remember soon after I got there, two guys came in frothing at the mouth and carrying on, one guy from the fire control group, one guy from the navigation group. They were both developing sub-systems which had to talk to each other, and this guy wouldn't tell the other guy, how he has going to get that signal over to him. He was afraid somebody was going to get in his area, and he was going to do something to control him.

Many, many weapon systems have been developed by the Navy, and many of them don't work simply because of this. I don't know why people don't understand it. Also, the fact that you can pull in all these experts to make it work in development and then when you get that job done, all these guys say, "Well, I've done my job," and walk away from it, and somebody else is going to produce the thing, you see. That's the wrong way, absolutely the wrong way. If you can make all these decisions you want in a development program and have such terrible impacts when you try to produce it—

Take the Terrier. They couldn't produce anything because they had a bunch of R&D guys doing it. I think we talked of that the last time. They had to redo the whole thing. I've found over the years that no thought is given to how you're going to deploy the thing, how you're going to support the thing, how you're going to maintain it and then how you're going to again get it back up on the line when you're doing overhauls and things of this sort. None of that has been thought through and wasn't going to be thought through. Again, these are the kinds of areas I'm trying to look at and started to look at: how to bring them together as a team, set up a system of disciplines within SP that would control that, bring them together, and find the program for them. These guys get the technical job done, you see, but don't let it die on the vine once you get it out there.

John T. Mason, Jr.: It's a matter of setting it up and also a matter of personalities, isn't it?

Mr. Buescher: Yes. As I said, we had a bunch of tigers. Something had to be done. I'm not sure that I did this, really thought all this through. There was a problem, and we had to solve it, and one thing led to another.

John T. Mason, Jr.: And you worked at it day by day.

Mr. Buescher: Fought it day by day and came up with the disciplines that were necessary. I'll say one thing—my bosses went along with everything I proposed, as long as they were reasonable, because it had to be done. Certainly Raborn couldn't get into that level of detail, and Levering couldn't get into that level of detail and set it up. So I felt that was my job, pulling them together as a team, set up the discipline necessary, to find the program and think of the long-term impact and the long-term management of that program.

Another thing was that our charter said, "We're going to develop that thing, and they're going to dissolve us." The organization had a very limited life. I don't know if you knew that

John T. Mason, Jr.: No. Dwell on that

John B. Buescher, Interview #2 (1/28/82) – Page 58

Mr. Buescher: Well, the charter just said we would develop; it didn't say anything about us being the support activity in the production area or the deployment area or maintain it or anything else. We had a limited charter. The idea was that there had been so many people throughout the Navy who fought against this type of organization that all they could say is, "We're just going to develop and get back in the normal way of doing things." That wouldn't work. There wasn't anybody you could turn it over to except us after it was all over with. We had all the background, we had the thing down the line, you see. You could not turn that over, and then it became evident as time went on.

John T. Mason, Jr.: But you were actually on trial, weren't you?

Mr. Buescher: We were on trial.

John T. Mason, Jr.: Was this Burke's idea?[*]

Mr. Buescher: I don't know. That's just the way the charter read. Maybe this was just simply because of the way things were going, the general attitude of things. They didn't worry about trying to think it through. They just wanted to get the job done, and it would work out, you see. It's probably just as well, because they'd just have that many more fights to set up the charter.

John T. Mason, Jr.: Somewhere along the line, are you going to talk about Raborn's role?

Mr. Buescher: Yes. I thought maybe you had all that.

John T. Mason, Jr.: But from your point of view. He told me himself.

Mr. Buescher: Raborn was and is a very dynamic person.[†] He was a hell of a good organizer in the sense that he knew how to go about getting support, getting money from

---

[*] Admiral Arleigh A. Burke, USN, served as Chief of Naval Operations from 17 August 1955 to 1 August 1961. He did a specialized oral history on Polaris for the Naval Institute collection.
[†] Vice Admiral Raborn died on 6 March 1990, several years after this interview.

the right people. And he had a personality that people warmed up to, very friendly, a very good guy. I think it was absolutely invaluable that they put a guy like that as head of it, because he didn't let any closed doors stop him. He had a job, and he went right into it but did it in a nice way. But he never let them stop and pushed the hell out of all of us and said, "Go ahead and get things done." And he'd go out and see what the Air Force was doing, and if he thought that was a good, he'd say, "Man, we ought to have something like that." Or he'd go out and see somebody with an idea for something and he'd go out and bring that idea back.

A lot of times all those great things that people presented to him were a lot of shit, so we had to sort out the pieces, you see. Sometimes I'd irritate the hell out of him, and any time there was an expert, he'd hire him and put him on the staff somewhere to help us. That was great. There wasn't any door that was closed to us in any way at any time, and I think that Raborn was responsible for that. He's very dynamic and could see the problem, go and present the problem to people that should know in order to make their decision up the line. He could present it at their level of knowledge and could get the job done.

John T. Mason, Jr.: He had those Saturday meetings.

Mr. Buescher: They were Saturday meetings. I don't know why he said it was a Saturday. We worked Saturdays for many years and sometimes Sundays unless he felt that so many people were traveling so much all the time that that's the only time he could really get them. I don't know. They were still having them when I got there. Sometime along the way—I don't remember when—we quit having them on Saturday. I guess a lot of contractors and a lot of government activities were not working on Saturday but SP, and he could gather his whole staff together at one time.

John T. Mason, Jr.: I got that idea that the people from the outside could come on Saturday without interrupting their weekly routine.

Mr. Buescher: That's right. Also, if the company wasn't working, then our guys weren't using up their time working with those individuals and those companies or government activities.

John T. Mason, Jr.: Nevertheless, the fact that you got together once a week was a tremendous—

Mr. Buescher: That's right. And those meetings have continued today, Monday morning meetings. It has a different content now. It's sort of management by exception, and the people that report, report on whether they have any problems. And you depend fully on them to tell whether they've got problems. If they say they don't have problems, that's it. There's nothing you can hide. A guy has to be honest; if he's not, he's really going to get himself in a bind. Does he need to direct his help? Does he need help outside of SP that he is unable to get? At one time there was also a lot of technical exchange on the Monday morning meetings or the Saturday meetings. That's when the group was small. Over the years and once we got the first one deployed, it came down to more about what was the status of our contract and what was the status of the money and what was the status of the people and what was the status of the technical program, and were there any problems.

John T. Mason, Jr.: The system was organized at that point; it was an ongoing thing and one evolved into the next one.

Mr. Buescher: I remember one of the first things; I hadn't been at SP but a couple of months. Up to that time, Air Force pretty much had the strategic weapons program of the country, although the Army had a responsibility for the land-based Jupiter. They had produced these big missiles, and for some reason Raborn felt he needed to get us to know these people better. He loaded his whole staff on a Navy plane and took them out to L.A., where the headquarters was. All of us went. By God, all of us went out there, and we heard these speeches. It's still part of that being able to work with people, getting them to accept us as part of the community whether we needed that or not. You just don't ignore them, you see.

John T. Mason, Jr.: The physical presence.

Mr. Buescher: Physical presence. I don't know that they did a bit of good except those things that you can't measure. I don't think it did much good that I'm aware of in development, although from time to time we would call on them if they had some technology we thought would be helpful to us. In that way, yes, it opened the gate. I think General Shriver was heading up the Air Force group.

John T. Mason, Jr.: He was.

Mr. Buescher: Well, Admiral Raborn felt it was worth it, something to be gained in the project, and if that was the case, by God, we were going to do it. We all went out, and we had the presentations, and we looked around at things and came on back and did our job.

John T. Mason, Jr.: Had Gordon Pehrson come on the scene at that point?[*]

Mr. Buescher: Yes. Gordon was there. I always felt that my relationship with Gordon was that we were not on the same frequency.

John T. Mason, Jr.: Wasn't he more a PR type?

Mr. Buescher: He was a budget type, management type.

John T. Mason, Jr.: But highly visible.

Mr. Buescher: Highly visible and very audible. He did a lot of good. He prodded Raborn into many things. I don't want to talk about people, but we just didn't agree in many cases. But Gordon was a good manager, no question about it. As long as he stayed out of the technical area, he was all right. Many of the branch heads fought him tooth and nail, because they felt that he was stepping on their toes. Of course, Gordon was trying to set up a reporting system.

---

[*] The recollections of Gordon O. Pehrson are in the Naval Institute oral history volume on the Polaris program.

John T. Mason, Jr.: That was the PERT system?*

Mr. Buescher: Well, PERT came later. So there was a lot of friction there. As a matter of fact, when I got there, Gordon's organization was known as SP north, and the technical group was known as SP south. You can see the division.

John T. Mason, Jr.: Ne'er the twain shall meet.

Mr. Buescher: We got things going. It was quite an organization I went into, you see.

John T. Mason, Jr.: Maybe now you should tell me about how you went about your role, as you saw your role with your—

Mr. Buescher: Well, initially, when I first arrived, I didn't really see the whole role; I just saw part of it. There were many problems—organization and technical—that came up. What was needed most was to get the organization to settle down and work as a team, rather than as many highly independent groups. I felt that we had to do something to pull it together. I felt that something had to be done so these programs could proceed toward a already understood goal, everybody understanding what their requirements were and what they had to do, rather than just kind of leave it up to each guy and say, "I'm doing my job."

So I set up a coordination program in which I took the lead in bringing about this coordination of these groups, first in identifying their requirements, what had to be coordinated between the groups to define our goals in understandable times. Secondly, to identify what had to be done to identify them and to get agreement as to what they were. I'm talking about maybe a little dimension, a chemical dimension, or it may be an operational requirement or may be an electrical requirement or may be anything wherever there was an interface, you see. Write it down, make them sign off on it, and then take control of those agreed interfaces and not let anyone make a change until they come back up the line.

---

* PERT--Program Evaluation Review Technique, a system of milestones for tracking the progress of a program against its schedule.

John T. Mason, Jr.: That's a difficult thing at that point.

Mr. Buescher: Yes, very difficult. And it didn't happen overnight. The first thing SP did was to run a series of feasibility studies. We had had all these studies during the steering task group deliberations, which began the first week after I reported. The steering task group was a group set up to try to bring thoughts together as to what a solid propellant system would be, the major parameters. They did their job, really with Levering Smith and Grayson Merrill running it and making the major decisions with the many people of the STG advising.* There were very excellent people on that crew.

John T. Mason, Jr.: Who selected them? Raborn?

Mr. Buescher: Raborn, yes. They reported to Raborn. Raborn had Levering Smith running the STG. So the general parameters of the system were established, but that's not enough. These are general parameters, you see. We had to take those requirements and get it down into a level of detail that people could use as a baseline for their development. We had to iterate those general requirements into detailed and specific goals. I ran an accuracy study and came up with an apportionment of accuracy goals for each subsystem.

John T. Mason, Jr.: That must have been a tedious task.

Mr. Buescher: A tedious task, and I believe it was the first time it had been done, frankly,

John T. Mason, Jr.: What kind of help did you have for that?

Mr. Buescher: We had anybody we could call on, but I had a contractor who understood these type of things pretty well and could provide immediate coordination for the study.

John T. Mason, Jr.: You mean a commercial contractor?

---

* STG—steering task group.

Mr. Buescher: Yes. Vitro, West Orange, helped me in that study and also the SP chief scientist helped. We came up with a specification that not only did this, and we didn't give it to them in these terms. For instance, if the requirement was that navigation had to meet an accuracy in so many nautical miles or parts of nautical miles, we didn't give the requirement to them that way. We gave it to them in terms of signals and information they had to generate and transmit next to the fire control group, so it was something we could measure. We didn't just give them a general number. We said, "You've got to locate north within such and such an accuracy, you've got to have speed over the ground within such and such an accuracy," these type of parameters, something we could measure, you see. We could hold them responsible and look at it as time went on as a development program.

John T. Mason, Jr.: That was a brilliant approach.

Mr. Buescher: It was, and Levering Smith was deeply involved in this. We also did the same thing with reliability, and in all other parameters. We specified launch forces, we specified shock requirements, for instance, and environment requirements, and we specified what level they would be outside the boat and to what level the launcher would have to protect the missile. We specified even the number of people they could count on in the submarine on patrol, being able to be available to operate and maintain that weapon system. We went into all the factors about it, and we put it out in a specification-type document which we imposed on the branches and the contractors as goals.

This was very important, and Levering Smith never let these be rigid requirements; he always made them goals. Why? People get so wrapped up in requirements; and if you say, "You have agreed under your contract to meet this requirement," then this becomes a rigid legal requirement and could result in considerable costs and time delays to fully meet each requirement. What we needed was arrangements that were more flexible, something that gave the technical director the opportunity to trade off between the different subsystems to make up for underachievement in one subsystem with overachievement of meeting goals in another system. By calling them "goals," this provided the opportunity to take such actions without long contractual hassles.

John T. Mason, Jr.: How long did this take?

Mr. Buescher: I think we took a few months, and in the meantime development had proceeded. I think probably we'd been in business six or eight months before we got it out on the street.

John T. Mason, Jr.: Did the whole group know that this was being developed at the time? This was reported?

Mr. Buescher: Yes, we kept putting it out in draft form. We'd never put out one of these things without bringing the whole team in and letting them see what we were doing and get their comment and help. We didn't just arbitrarily impose a new document on them like this. Sometimes we were off base, and they'd tell us. That was great; that's what we wanted to know.

John T. Mason, Jr.: There's a tremendous amount of psychology employed in this.

Mr. Buescher: I guess there is. But that was a good document, very fine, and it formed a written baseline in terms that we in the technical division could understand and Raborn could understand and everybody throughout the program could understand and say, "That's what I've got to do; that's my job."

That wasn't enough, though. That was just a start. Now, you get down on a day-by-day basis, you now bring in hundreds and thousands of engineers, design engineers who've got to design the equipments, each part and who've got to make studies of parts, parameters, to see if things fit together functionally and physically, who've got to look at the whole equipment. There has to be some way of controlling and identifying where the weapon system goals and requirements override or control his detail design and the constraints placed on his design.

Navy experience has shown that too often equipments and subsystems arrive at a shipyard, and they won't work when installed in a ship and will not interface with requirements and subsystems furnished by other contractors. The reason that they do not work together is often the result from a lack of controls of the characteristics of each side of the interface. The interface may be a mechanical fit, an electrical signal transmitted by one subsystem and received by another subsystem, or it may be many other types of interfacing characteristic. There is a serious need to control the interface, so that equipments are properly designed. If equipment is then delivered and it won't interface, it can be quickly determined who is at fault. So we set up this coordination program, a rather detailed coordination of all the detailed interface parameters throughout the entire weapon system.

John T. Mason, Jr.: To sit on top of this whole thing at all times.

Mr. Buescher: Yes. After we had gone through identifying what had to be done, what things had to be controlled and had come to an agreement on each, these were documented on a set of drawings called coordination drawings. Each SP branch had to initial off each drawing to indicate concurrence, and then I authenticated their drawing by my signature. When they couldn't come to agreement, I would make the decision or I'd carry it up the line for decision if I felt it necessary. Agreement on these detailed parameters never came easily, and many involved long, drawn-out studies, discussions, and battles.

People would say, "Why don't you just go ahead and make that decision for them? Tell them what to do." It is much faster. That way, I would make the decision if they couldn't eventually agree. But what I wanted to do was to force the subsystem branches/contractors to bite the bullet and come to an agreement in each case. We would have these large coordination meetings attended by SP and contractor personnel, other Navy commands, and their contractors, at which everything was brought out. Everybody's problems were discussed. As a team what we were doing was make each team member realize that something was on the other side of the interface. If a solution required a trade-off on each side of the interface to resolve problems, they should have some understanding of the other fellow's problems and to help us make that trade-off.

John T. Mason, Jr.: It seems to me you were running against a very human problem. So many men do not have that ability to make a positive decision.

Mr. Buescher: We found that out. And often this was the type of detail that was shuttled down to the lower level of the organization, because that's where the detailed design is done. We'd bring it up to top management, if it was necessary to go to the top, particularly if there was a great impact. We aired the thing; we publicized it so everybody understood what was happening.

Originally there was reluctance on people's part to become involved in this program, but as time went and as each new generation of weapon system was delivered, this program was more and more.

John T. Mason, Jr.: How big was your staff?

Mr. Buescher: In Polaris it never got over—there were two more guys helping me.

John T. Mason, Jr.: Two?

Mr. Buescher: Two more.

John T. Mason, Jr.: Handpicked?

Mr. Buescher: Handpicked. I think now for Trident I, I had a group of seven established to do the job. I could have had more, but that's all I needed. You can get too many people for a job. We were not trying to do the job ourselves. We were running the program, making sure the trade-offs were made, making sure it was understood, making sure that what was written on the paper, what tied it down, was clear and not ambiguous, and we were scheduling the whole thing. We had excellent support from Vitro, who was my contractor.

John T. Mason, Jr.: Even though you had a staff and it was small, when you relied on them, you had to be on top of the whole thing.

Mr. Buescher: Yes. Also we had originally contracted with Vitro because over the years they had provided some weapon system support for NavOrd.* However, as we all learned they did quite a different job for us than they had done for BuOrd. Our way of running the program was quite different and new.

John T. Mason, Jr.: They grew with the project too?

Mr. Buescher: Yes. We developed this whole new concept. Even today, the rest of Vitro does business completely different, completely different and the relationships between SP and Vitro are much closer and friendlier and were allowed to exercise much more initiative. The other way, there's an adversary arrangement but not in our program. Vitro people were part of the team. They work very closely with us and are very proud to be such an intimate part of the program, because we got things done. We are very glad to have them as our supporting contractor.

John T. Mason, Jr.: That was the thing that brought that into focus.

Mr. Buescher: In the early days of the program I had a few run-ins with other parts of Vitro Corporation, because I felt they were undermining the position of our support group at Vitro. There was another part of Vitro who was in the hardware business, and they felt they had the capability to bid on and produce training devices for SP, in competition with the SP subsystem contractors. They would bid on these devices, and I took them off the bidder's list. I told them I did it. Oh, we had a round, so I gave them the option: "You do it that way, or you do it my way. If you do it your way, you don't have a contract with me, but if you do it my way then we'll continue." So the cooler heads at Vitro ruled, and the other parts of Vitro never tried to bid on anything with SP in competition with the SP subsystem contractors.

The reason for my concern is this: Vitro, as my staff, had access to all of our

---

* NavOrd—Naval Ordnance Systems Command, which existed from 1966 until it was consolidated with the Naval Ship Systems Command in 1974 to form the Naval Sea Systems Command.

contractors and their information, not like any other contractor in the program. They were able to gain access, to gain information on each different subsystem, going to the different subsystem contractor's plant. In many cases they were privy to contractor-owned information and sensitive information. To be credible and for this information to continue to be given to them, they had to be most careful on how they used this information. Certainly they could never compete with the subsystem contractors for contracts. For some reason, the other part of Vitro didn't understand it, because they came up in the old BuOrd system. They would have been completely ineffective in weapon coordination had I let them go ahead in the example mentioned above; they were bidding against one of our subsystem contractors, by the way. GE wanted to do the job, and they were very capable of doing it, so Vitro said, "I want it too."[*] But they didn't get it ever. They got out of the hardware business with SP.

John T. Mason, Jr.: Would you John, go off on this tangent at the moment and talk about the contractors as a group and their contribution and your relationship with them?

Mr. Buescher: Well, the technical division in SP is made up of seven technical branches, SP 22, launcher; SP 23, fire control and guidance; SP 24, navigation; SP 25, test groups. The test groups primarily ran the ranges and test ships. SP 26 was ships subsystem with the naval liaison and had contact with the NavSea group who built the ship, and SP 27 had the missiles. Each of those groups had a subsystem contractor supporting him. They were responsible for that subsystem. At the division level—and I'm talking about the technical division—there was the director. At that time it was Levering Smith and later Bob Gooding, Bob Wertheim, and Glen Clark.[†] I was chief engineer, as well as a deputy to the technical director.

---

[*] GE—General Electric.
[†] Rear Admiral Robert C. Gooding, USN, served as Commander Naval Ship Systems Command from 1972 to 1974. As a vice admiral, he served as Commander Naval Sea Systems Command from 1974 to 1976. Rear Admiral Robert H. Wertheim, USN, served as director of the Strategic Systems Project Office from 14 November 1977 to 1 November 1980. Rear Admiral Glenwood Clark, Jr., USN, served as director of the Strategic Systems Project Office/Strategic Systems Program Office from 1 November 1980 to 20 June 1985.

I had a staff, we had a management staff, a small one, and we had our contractors who reported directly to us. I had Vitro primarily. I had some government activities working for me that we'll talk about that later, and I had NOL Corona working to support the quality control and reliability programs. We had APL, who assisted in the evaluations of the weapon system, and we had other people from time to time, such as people involved in human engineering.

John T. Mason, Jr.: What was his name?

Mr. Buescher: I've forgotten his name. He was one of the guys that Raborn picked up, and he was to help us out.

John T. Mason, Jr.: Dr. Jack Dunlap.

Mr. Buescher: We provided the overall pulling together of the system. Unlike many of the Air Force systems, we didn't have a systems contractor. We were the systems contractor. Vitro and APL and people like that had absolutely no directive authority; they were people who helped us run our program, us being at the systems level. That's why it was so important that they have access to all these contractors and contractors' information. They did a tremendous amount of work to help us get these things done, but they were always a staff support to us and we made the decisions.

John T. Mason, Jr.: There was a group of contractors who you had involved. Chrysler was the prominent one, I think, when the Jupiter program was still—

Mr. Buescher: That's right.

John T. Mason, Jr.: And then that was all done away with and you got your own different contractors.

Mr. Buescher: That's right. When we changed over to the solid-propellant Polaris, we got a whole brand-new set of contractors.

John T. Mason, Jr.: What was the wisdom in back of that?

Mr. Buescher: Well, we got people who knew how to do a specific job. For instance, Lockheed had a group of people who had been involved in high-altitude testing of reentry bodies and had a good design group. They understood the problem, and it was on that group that we built and selected a missile subsystem contractor. GE had been in the fire control business all these years for BuOrd. We took a group of those people at GE and projecticized them and used that expertise to bring it into our program. They understood naval systems. Chrysler did not; Chrysler understood the Jupiter system and the things that the Army was doing, but they didn't understand naval ordnance systems. It was the same thing throughout. That's why each of these contractors was selected.

But Raborn insisted that the people and effort at that contractor plant be projecticized for the Polaris program so that we would not share our people or management of the people in the contractor's plant. They would be a separate group reporting to and responsible only to us. It was an excellent way to get their attention and keep their attention. So that's the way they came about, and that's the way they were selected. Each of them had a nucleus of a group of people with an excellent capability to do the necessary job.

I think another real important point is that SP and its contractors had cradle-to-grave responsibility for the system. I told you earlier that our charter didn't include any of that, but we quickly realized that you couldn't do only an R&D job; you had to use the same group of people. In other words, we were not going to develop it and turn it over to another group. All the development and production, QC, maintenance responsibility were in the same group of people.[*] It was not divided.

John T. Mason, Jr.: And when was this wisdom apparent to you people?

Mr. Buescher: Early in the program, very early in the program.

---

[*] QC—quality control.

John T. Mason, Jr.: Did you have to go to higher authorities?

Mr. Buescher: No. Levering Smith had a lot to do with it.

John T. Mason, Jr.: You just assumed it?

Mr. Buescher: Yes, we just assumed that was the way we were going to do it. Raborn thought that was the way to go, so that's the way it was set up. Too often, as I said before, you can do so many things in the development program, and if you do not consider the effects these have downstream, you may not be able to produce or maintain the equipment.

John T. Mason, Jr.: How soon did the various bureaus come around to acceptance of this point of view?

Mr. Buescher: Not immediately. I got into a number of fights. For instance, as time went on, we got worried about quality control, and I began to do things to set up a quality control organization and quality control requirement. I didn't have any trouble with the quality control people in BuOrd. I had trouble with the personnel people who showed up en masse in my office one day.

John T. Mason, Jr.: Civil service people?

Mr. Buescher: Civil service people within the BuOrd, people who were providing support. They felt that I wasn't doing it right, and they were going to tell me how. Well, we had a shouting contest, and I threw them out of the office. Then we went ahead and did it the way we wanted to do it.

I think on the coordination drawings I've tried to explain the purpose and the scope. The scope included every type of interface. I would say that today we must have 20,000 drawings, big drawings full of these requirements that we'd coordinate. We did it for each subsystem for the submarines, for each class of submarines, for each class of missile, surface ships such as the tenders. We even did it for some of the test ships where there was a need to get this kind of control. We have done it for the test facilities where people have to work together and work things out like at Cape Canaveral, the installations down there. It's a very, very extensive program. As I told you before, people fought it at first. I found that as time went on, it became more and more accepted, and I was the one that said, "Don't overdo this thing because you can tie yourself in knots." It became a very accepted program.

John T. Mason, Jr.: The very success of the program.

Mr. Buescher: People saw that it helped them, whereas before they were very suspicious of it, very suspicious of it.

John T. Mason, Jr.: And you had that overriding political consideration, too, the imperative nature of the program, national defense.

Mr. Buescher: That's right, but it seemed like personalities more than that were driving the objections. Let me just tell you something else. The next thing, I guess, to come up—you can't run this type of program, and you can't go into production if you don't have good design disclosure and design disclosure, drawing specifications for things of this sort, even process control, which controls it in detail, and you have a way of controlling changes. Always people want to make a lot of changes; they always want to make it better, and they'll improve it to death so it doesn't work.

John T. Mason, Jr.: There has to be a cut-off time, doesn't there?

Mr. Buescher: There comes a time, but when you say you have to freeze a drawing, I mean freeze them, absolutely freeze them and have a change control system which would really limit the changes and bring it under government control. That's the way we've done it. We talk about detail down to the piece parts level in each of our subsystems. So that was the next thing I started beating on to get done and get done right—to come up with a complete set of documentation, come up with a change control system that would control it and to put our field reps, which we had in the major contractor business, essentially in charge of that—with the branch responsible, too, on a day-by-day basis—and to delegate the authority to sign off the drawing when the proper time comes. The proper time is about the time you have gone into production and you have accepted the first item, whatever that item may be. It may be a sub-assembly, assembly; it may be a complete missile. You do it gradually as times goes on, as these things are first presented for inspection, to gradually work up this whole set of drawings and freeze it as it goes on. So that was the next thing to come up, first with a full set of documentation and then have rigid conformance to that.

John T. Mason, Jr.: You couldn't have any weak links in your rep system.

Mr. Buescher: No, we had very good reps and they had good staffs, good, hard-working guys.

John T. Mason, Jr.: How were they selected?

Mr. Buescher: How do you select a naval officer? How do you select those officers in SP? Simply because you dig around through the records and go around and talk to people and see who are the capable guys and then get them. That's the way it's done. You don't depend on BuPers to give you these guys.[*]

John T. Mason, Jr.: No, I would think not.

Mr. Buescher: You don't. As a matter of fact, you do everything in the world to step in and keep them from assigning people until you already know who it is and you know who they are and you've already checked them out.

So as time went on, we began to set up and document this full-design disclosure that we're talking about, not just how to build something, but where there's a critical

---

[*] BuPers—Bureau of Naval Personnel.

process, to write that up and freeze that process so they can't change the process on you. Again, some of this stuff is witchcraft, particularly in the propellant business, and it's how you handle it and how you process it that has as much to do with it as what's the formulation and how you fabricate these things.

So where critical process is involved, fix on that so they can't change it. You've got your development contractor preparing these documents whose design engineers are working on it day by day. They are going to have to check this thing off, and the SP plant reps were working along with them on a day-by-day basis in order to come up with a complete set of documentation in all the areas. We also had to come up with inspection documentation which was part of the package, so you know how to inspect for it and whether there are critical things or not.

John T. Mason, Jr.: You must have had some problems along the way.

Mr. Buescher: A very detailed process. Some SP people who had never been in such a controlled system had problems, particularly those guys whose background and experience was not ordnance design. The ordnance guys had had background, but some of our subsystems were terrible, and it took a lot of meetings with these guys to get it in line, both with the people in the branches and the contractors. The contractors weren't going to do any more than they were forced to do, and the branches weren't doing their job right.

That's where it started, except in one case, trying to get one of the branches and one of the contractors set up to do the job and do this job right, we'd meet and agree on what would be done, a few months later we'd meet and nothing had happened, nothing. So one day I went to tell Levering I was having so much trouble, and he said, "Bypass the branch, go to the contractor," and that ended it. So I wrote up a message to them and gave them hell, and they began to get in line. Levering said to bypass the branch, don't fool with them, bypass them. They didn't understand how to do it, and I did, and everything worked out fine.

John T. Mason, Jr.: Did they come around after having been bypassed?

Mr. Buescher: They got it in line, and finally we got the documentation, and we got change control systems set up. We got our field office in a position to have something to work with. We got it in line.

John T. Mason, Jr.: That must have entailed a great deal of activity on your part and you must have had to go places.

Mr. Buescher: I did. I did quite a bit of travel.

John T. Mason, Jr.: Put out a fire here. Can you recall any of those experiences?

Mr. Buescher: Yes. As time went on—and this was not A-1 Polaris; it was a little bit further down the line—we set up a group to evaluate quality control systems, and we went to two or three of our contractors.* It turned out to be a rather unbiased judgment, although the people on it you would have thought would have been rather biased people, because we were the ones who had been beating on them, but it turned out that we got some good outside help. One of the guys was Dr. Juran, who is one of the real experts in quality control in this country. There are two guys in this country who are credited with making the Japanese quality control conscious, and he is one of them. He was with the Japanese for years, and they did anything he told them to do.

John T. Mason, Jr.: That boomeranged, didn't it?

Mr. Buescher: Absolutely outstanding quality control.

John T. Mason, Jr.: That boomeranged as far as we're concerned.

Mr. Buescher: Right. But he is a well-known fellow. We went to missile contractors, we went to navigation contractors, and we brought about some rather major changes in the

---

* The first version of the submarine-launched Polaris ballistic missile, the A-1, was 28 feet long, 4 feet in diameter, and weighed about 30,000 pounds. It had a range of 1,200 nautical miles. The missile entered fleet service in 1960 in the nuclear-powered submarine George Washington (SSBN-598).

organization and the attitudes of the contractors. In some cases it was very welcomed by them, and in some cases it wasn't, but they all got in line very well.

John T. Mason, Jr.: And underneath all of that was activity on your part to get them in line.

Mr. Buescher: Yes. Of course, up the line they were very anxious in SP—Levering and Raborn—to get this squared away and get these things right. So it was a very detailed effort. We'd make several trips over a period of two or three months and be gone a couple of weeks at a time to really get into the details, and we had real cooperation to bring about changes, so that was really great.

What we tried to do with all this is to come up with a uniformity of configuration, like I told you we always had in the ammunition program. We were trying the same thing here, you see. When you produce one, it's representative of the whole bit. We needed a system to control. At first we didn't have a system; we didn't have any of these things. We knew we were not bound by any of the ways that anybody else had done it, and we set up our own system for doing it. For example, there were systems within BuOrd called ordalts—ordnance alterations. There were systems within BuShips called shipalts, very cumbersome systems with general control, nobody really running the thing. We wanted something more specific. We wanted all of our missiles uniform. Say if it was an A-1 missile, we wanted all of our A-1 missiles to be just alike, those out in the fleet and those in stock. If it was fire control, we wanted all of our fire control to be alike in every ship. In navigation, it was the same way. If we made a change of missiles or we made a change in class of a boat with the new equipment, then we wanted all of that to be the same.

We came up with a system of SP alterations, which we called SP-alts. The system provided a very, very detailed management of the change program. All these SP-alts had to come up and be signed by the technical director. We did not leave it up to the branches and to the field activities and the contractors to make these changes once the equipment was operational. What happens is when you make an operational change, all of your documentation—not only your design documentation, but all of the fleet documentation, training of the crews, spare parts, provision—all that can be affected.

So many systems in the Navy that are not working today are not working simply because they don't think all this through beforehand. Our system required that you go through and look at the spare parts picture, the provisioning picture, change the technical documentation before you introduce that SP-alt into the fleet. All these things that were necessary to operate and maintain that system were to be done beforehand, and that's the major difference. First, it was a complete system and second, we maintained control with the SP division at the division level. Every SP-alt came through me. I checked it out for effective coordination, documented spare parts, and all this, to make sure all of these things were done, to see that the branch and the contractor had done it. And then I would pass it on up to the technical director, and he would approve or disapprove it.

John T. Mason, Jr.: We had this advantage that it was a new project and everything evolved there.

Mr. Buescher: It evolved there.

John T. Mason, Jr.: It wasn't something or a way of managing that had been begun by some other group and you took it over.

Mr. Buescher: That's right. We were able to do what we felt was necessary, and in most cases we did not try to adopt existing systems because they didn't fit. That SP-alt system is still in effect today. People say it's a slow system. Yes, it can be very fast as any other system if we wanted it to go through. It is a slow system, and it'll slow them down and keep them from changing something to death so it never works. We require proofing of that SP-alt to show that it works. In case of changes to the missile, we required that it be proved in flight testing, and we required for many cases that equipment be sent back to the factory or one of our shore activities for SP-alting, rather than let the fleet personnel do it.

One of the things we put our early in the program—that I wrote up and Levering issued—was a maintenance policy which formed the basis for the design of our equipment. Previously the way maintenance had been done was to depend heavily on the crew and crew skills to keep it up, to make changes—particularly in electronics—to put in new pieces where maybe the resistor failed or maybe a module. Our requirement was to design for module replacement. A module is a board with a lot of these little parts and pieces, transistors and resistors on them. We let that be a unity and try to fix the system by replacing the modules, send those modules back to a shore facility where we have configuration control and where people are trained better. We have control over the parts that go into them, and you don't take a substitute part out of the supply system. That can kill you. If they don't have it, they say, "Well, this book says this is equivalent, so we'll use that." That doesn't go. Or to tweak the things to make it work in that installation. But it won't work in all the others. You can screw up a missile real fast that way.

John T. Mason, Jr.: I'm sure you can. How did this wisdom develop?

Mr. Buescher: Simply because we had a situation where we had two crews.[*] One of them goes out for 60 days and comes back; another crew takes over. You can't have things written down on the back of envelopes and in people's heads. You have to be able to turn over a working system, and that's the only way we could figure this thing out. Doing it by modular replacement, train them to do that; don't let them get in there and mess up all this stuff with substitute parts. When we make a change, give them the new documentation and new spare parts to go with it, and they can deal with it.

John T. Mason, Jr.: That system developed well along.

Mr. Buescher: It developed early, so it was reflected in the design.

John T. Mason, Jr.: I see.

Mr. Buescher: It's sort of out of sequence of how that came about, but it's part of this discipline we were developing as time goes on.

---

[*] As the concept for the ballistic submarines developed, a key decision was to provide each submarine with two complete crews, a blue crew and a gold crew. That enabled each submarine to spend a maximum amount of time on deterrent patrols while the off-duty crew members spent time with their families and took shore-based training.

John T. Mason, Jr.: Did this have some influence on Rickover's insistence on the training and so forth?*

Mr. Buescher: Absolutely none. None. He did his thing and we did our thing.

John T. Mason, Jr.: But they seem to mesh in ideas.

Mr. Buescher: I'm not fully familiar with their system, but they and we are about the only Navy system that really control in this depth of detail. We control the interfaces between the systems, we are controlling how the contractors design the equipment for maintenance, the level of maintenance we are controlling, we are controlling the system for controlling design changes or changes in manufacture. All of that is coming back up to the division level for approval. It wasn't just a bunch of papers coming through to get signed off; they really got worked over.

John T. Mason, Jr.: It's a remarkable, remarkable achievement because in one sense it goes contrary to the individuals.

Mr. Buescher: That's right, the individual delegation of authority.

John T. Mason, Jr.: The individuality is submerged into this whole thing.

Mr. Buescher: That's right. We're looking at it from a system level; it wasn't but one system. These other people were subsystems, and they had to work as part of the system.

The next thing that happened is you send all of this equipment to the shipyard and get it installed and try to get it to work in a submarine, you see. Up to that time, the way in the Terrier and I guess the Talos program, what happened was all this equipment would be

---

* Hyman G. Rickover was considered the father of the nuclear Navy. He ran the U.S. Navy's nuclear-power program for many years, from 1948 until he eventually left active duty in 1982 with the rank of four-star admiral on the retired list. Rickover Hall at the Naval Academy is named in his honor, as is the nuclear-powered attack submarine Hyman G. Rickover (SSN-709), which was commissioned 21 July 1984.

shipped to the shipyard for installation in the ship.* Although the shipbuilders could build the ship and they could make it act like and do everything a ship ought to do, they couldn't get the weapons system working. They didn't have configuration control; they didn't have control of anything. So they would take that ship after it was completed, put it over in another shipyard and spend two or three years trying to make that weapon systems work. Lack of control, that's lack of control.

John T. Mason, Jr.: That's what Eli ran up against with the Canberra when he was skipper.†

Mr. Buescher: The Boston, the Canberra.

John T. Mason, Jr.: The ship was all right, but the weapons systems—

Mr. Buescher: They did not have the disciplines to force things, you see. Now, as I told you, we had a set of coordination drawings. If anything was not working, we could go in and determine what was not working and who had screwed it up. It could be that the interface was wrong, but most of the time somebody had not met interface requirements.

John T. Mason, Jr.: You could put your finger on it right away.

Mr. Buescher: We could put our fingers on it. We set up a shipyard test program, again, managed out of SP, not by the shipbuilders to say what had to be tested, the tolerances they had to meet in tests to be acceptable, both along shore and at sea, including launching of missiles—not real missiles yet, because that's the next phase. I came up with a specification for all of this with the help of everybody involved. We set up a six-phase installation test program. Phase one and two—the shipbuilder puts in cabling, he puts in

---

* Talos was a long-range ramjet missile used by surface ships in the antiair mission. Its first successful intercept of a drone target was in October 1952. It entered fleet service on board the cruiser Galveston (CLG-3) in 1957 and from then until 1979 was the U.S. Navy's most impressive shipboard antiair missile.
† Captain Eli T. Reich, USN, commanded the guided missile heavy cruiser Canberra (CAG-2) from October 1960 to December 1961.

services, electrical, he puts in air-conditioning, he has to supply water at a certain temperature for cooling and heating. All the things he had to do were tested during phase one and two. We could check those out as he does them. We could check them for electrical continuity, for smoke tests, check them for level of voltage at the point it is to be delivered—not when he generates it, but when it is to be delivered.

Phase three and four had to do with the subsystem contractors, which our subsystems were involved in and responsible for. They tested these individual equipments after they were installed to see if they were operating properly in that environment and then as a subsystem, to see if the pieces of equipment talked to each other and operated as a subsystem the way they were checked out in the factory.

Then Phases five and six were the systems test, which came under me. The whole program was under me, but it was my job with SP 26 and Vitro to write those tests and say this was the way we were going to check it out. If they didn't meet the tolerances or if they wanted to change a test or the test conditions, we even specified who was going to witness the tests and what data all these details and made it a team effort in the shipyard. Everybody understood what the program was. These other boats that Eli was talking about, they never had anything like this. They never had any baseline to check it against and never had an organized system to check it out. It was under the control, usually, of the shipbuilder, and it's very difficult to transfer that knowledge over to the shipbuilder. He's worried about getting the ship built and less worried about the weapon system.

John T. Mason, Jr.: Shipbuilders, as I know them, are sometimes rather tough cookies. It must have taken some extra effort to get them to knuckle under to this system.

Mr. Buescher: It did. It took a lot of effort, but we introduced it very early in the program that we were going to do it this way. We were the project managers, and the shipbuilders got with it. I remember at one of the meetings when we went up to Eli to talk about this thing and make sure they understood what we were talking about. This was kind of a loud meeting, as you might expect.

John T. Mason, Jr.: Who was up there then? Was Shugg there then?*

Mr. Buescher: I've forgotten. We were not working at that level. We were working with the level of the guys who were in charge a couple of levels down. It had been going on for two or three days, and eventually the system just went into effect. But at that particular meeting, I remember Levering was up at EB for some other reason, and he said, "How's it going?" I told him about all these problems, and he said, "Let me go over there and get involved."

And I said, "Not yet, not yet, don't get involved yet; you're my last resort. I'm not ready for you to get into it." We got things settled finally without calling on Levering.

John T. Mason, Jr.: Waiting for the big guns to come in.

Mr. Buescher: SP assigned responsibilities to the supervisor of shipbuilding.† They double-hatted him, making him an SP agent reporting to Raborn. That helped. All these things helped to make them part of the family and to define their responsibilities. The management of the installation test program was retained in SP, and even today it's the same way. All of these things I'm telling you about in concept have not changed. We've improved them within the concept and generally the controls remain in effect today. That's 25 years.

John T. Mason, Jr.: That's remarkable again. What other shipbuilders besides Electric Boat were there?

Mr. Buescher: Newport News.

John T. Mason, Jr.: To a much lesser extent, though?

---

* Carleton Shugg was president of the Electric Boat Division of the General Dynamics Corporation. His recollections are in the Naval Institute oral history volume on the Polaris program.
† The supervisor of shipbuilding is a naval officer who is the Navy's on-scene representative to monitor the progress of construction and repair of Navy ships at commercial shipyards.

Mr. Buescher: They built quite a few ships. EB was always a design yard. Newport News was a follow-on construction yard.[*] The government shipyard was Mare Island.[†] Bremerton was overhaul.[‡] I've forgotten who else; there was another government shipyard that built some of our ships.[§] There had to be nuclear submarine shipyards first. There was Newport News, EB, Mare Island, Charleston. Charleston built tenders too.

John T. Mason, Jr.: Oh, yes, of course. We are talking about shipbuilding in a broader sense; you are talking about contractors. You might say something as an integral part of the story about the method of contracting and the need for breaking contracts sometimes when they didn't conform.

Mr. Buescher: In the early days, contracting was a very easy thing. Everybody was with us; everybody was pulling to get us going all for a cost plus fixed fee.

John T. Mason, Jr.: You didn't go through the normal government procedure of bidding and all that kind of thing, did you?

Mr. Buescher: We selected our family of contractors, and usually we kept those guys. As a matter of fact, the same family of contractors we had selected 25 years ago, we still have them today. Over the years there have been a lot of people who in their wisdom at different levels in the government have come up with all these fancy new ways of contracting, particularly pushing for competitive bidding. We've been lucky to be able to not have had to go into competition.

John T. Mason, Jr.: That's where politics enters into it.

Mr. Buescher: That's right. Not that it's policy, but our systems, A-1, A-2, A-3, C-3, C-4, D-5 are all evolutionary; they evolved from the one before. You've got a bunch of

---

[*] Newport News Shipbuilding and Dry Dock Company, a private shipyard.
[†] Mare Island Naval Shipyard, Vallejo, California.
[‡] Puget Sound Naval Shipyard, Bremerton, Washington.
[§] Portsmouth Naval Shipyard, Kittery, Maine, was also involved in SSBN construction.

contractors in support activities who have the knowledge and know what has to be done to get to the next generation of equipments. Rather than going into competition and having to start all over from scratch with new contractors, it's been a long, hard battle over the years to keep from having to go that route. As a matter of fact, even in the D-5, Congress and everybody else had gotten involved, and they didn't really understand about competition and what it does to you or what it doesn't do for you. There's been a hell of a battle to get that accepted.

John T. Mason, Jr.: That's what I suspected because the traditional way was the other.

Mr. Buescher: That's right. A lot of the money, an awful lot of the percentage of our money went into a multitude of contractors, but on subcontract. We've got our major subsystem contractors who help us manage the program as well as do the development and do the production. But they go out to a multitude of subcontractors. Sometimes it's directed to these people to develop in the development phase and in the production phase. We go where we can get the best support. But we primarily get competition contracting through our subsystem contractors, and that's awfully hard for a congressman to understand in a state where there's a lot of unemployment.

John T. Mason, Jr.: When he has some industry in his district that he wants a favor.

Mr. Buescher: That's exactly right. It's been a godsend to this program that we didn't have to make these changes of contractors each time, because that would mean starting all over and would be a terrible upset, a terrible upset, of the program.

John T. Mason, Jr.: It's rather remarkable however, that your system was imposed at the beginning.

Mr. Buescher: That's right.

John T. Mason, Jr.: When all these other ideas were not yet formulated completely, they were simply evolving, and yet this contract system was imposed at the beginning. Is that right?

Mr. Buescher: Yes, but we had to reestablish it every time this new generation came along. These things that I'm talking about, these disciplines—we could establish those and keep them going within our prerogative, but on this contracting system we had a lot of people on the outside trying to force it some other way. It was never easy to fight them off, you know, because from their viewpoint that's the correct thing to do. Like Alan Shepard said—you remember when he went up in the first space flight, he said he shuddered to think that this thing was made out of pieces of the lowest bidder, which doesn't mean the best quality.[*] He had something there.

John T. Mason, Jr.: Well, I suppose the other is the democratic approach to things, and this is much more central authority. Let's go back to maintenance now.

Mr. Buescher: Even though we said to do it by modular replacement, we put some fierce restrictions on what could be replaced. For instance, in the missile, we restricted it to a major package, something like that, a flight control package where you took it out and put another one in there. Don't touch the insides of it; just send it back to Lockheed, the contractor. We limited package replacement to that for which we had the capability to test and make sure we had gotten that replacement package back in the missile and it was operating in the missile.

John T. Mason, Jr.: This was innovative, wasn't it? Did this system exist anywhere else in industry?

Mr. Buescher: I don't know. A lot of people say, "Well, let's not do anything, let's not replace anything in the missile. Send back the whole missile." But we couldn't go along with that, make a wooden missile out of it. We've never accepted that. We still say we can

---

[*] On 5 May 1961 Commander Alan B. Shepard, USN, became the first American astronaut to fly into space. He completed a 15-minute sub-orbital flight in a Mercury spacecraft. After splashdown he was recovered by a helicopter and landed on the deck of the aircraft carrier Lake Champlain (CVS-39).

train the crews sufficiently to replace a major component, but we feel that we've got to be able to replace some of these like a guidance system. We say to the fleet, "You don't do anything to the guidance system. Pull it out and put another one in there, but don't do anything to it. Keep your hands off of it." These things are rather sophisticated, and you can't have every sailor who comes along who may or may not understand the system to make changes.

On something that's installed in the ship—such as fire control or navigation—where you can do a lot more testing, where you can do a lot more replacement and make sure in the testing afterwards that it is operating satisfactorily, we replaced blocks of modules. A signal may not be not coming in right; it's affected by these 50 modules. Take them out. Put 50 new ones in there that are good, out of the stock if that's what is needed in the missile countdown to get the fire control back on the line real fast. In some cases we've given them equipment to screen these modules, to test them individually, and if they're good, to put them back in their stock.

John T. Mason, Jr.: So they're not lost.

Mr. Buescher: No, they're not lost. Sometimes you can't do it that way, and a large part of them come back, ship them back. We set up our own repair facilities for this type of thing in Charleston, South Carolina, under our control, in which we have all our disciplines evoked there. We don't just send it to a general repair facility or anything of that sort. We're going to do it our way, under our controls.

John T. Mason, Jr.: I suppose that there's more expense involved in that system, but there's more assurance too.

Mr. Buescher: What's the system worth if you know it's not reliable? There are too many operational systems that are not reliable, and you can't depend on them. We've had an extremely, extremely high operational reliability with this system, and it's because of this type of disciplines and controls, I believe. At least it's had a major effect on it.

Well, let's go back to the quality control program.

John T. Mason, Jr.: First, let me ask has this system been adapted by industry now in many cases in the electronics field?

Mr. Buescher: Yes, in many cases. Even your TV, they replace modules now. They don't come out and replace resistors. You'll see this advertised. It's the way to go. Things are getting too complicated and too complex.

John T. Mason, Jr.: For the individual to be on top of

Mr. Buescher: I'm not very good at electronics, but I used to be able to do my own repair on my TV. I don't even open mine up anymore.

If it's bad, I call somebody to come out and fix it. He comes out, tests the set to determine a failed module, which he removes and puts another one in and goes away. That's the way my set is designed. It's a good system. It's expensive to replace a module.

John T. Mason, Jr.: That's what I wondered.

Mr. Buescher: Sometimes these things have to be balanced out, and you can't just put another part in there, particularly if its output is at the extreme of tolerance. It may not match with these other things and these things have to be matched and checked out as a module. The modules have a trade-in value. You get a certain amount of trade-in value on it, and they can go back and rework it and get it back in line.

John T. Mason, Jr.: I hope you don't mind my diverting you in cases like that.

Mr. Buescher: No, no.

John T. Mason, Jr.: I think these little facets to the story—

Mr. Buescher: No, real fine. In the early part of the program, we were all concerned about the quality we were going to get, and we had to do something—this was in the evolvement phase—to become more cost-conscious and quality-conscious and try to do things to get our contractors geared up for the production phase. There were some standard contractor government industry agreed specifications for quality control, the kinds of programs they would run, and things of this sort.

My guys and my support activities and I looked at this agreed specification, and we felt it was too loose, much too loose a system. We couldn't get the controls we needed, so we developed our own. Oh, we had a tough time. We had a terrible time with the industry guys, DoD guys; they didn't want us to do it. We kept saying, "We can't get the control we want under this system; it's too loose. We think there's a better way of doing it." So we developed our own set of specifications, signed it out, and imposed it on our contractors.

This system, like all the others I have talked about, had configuration control and documentation and coordination drawings as important elements in it. I had a group on my staff to manage that and monitor it and make sure that we were not just putting out directives and forgetting about them. That's too often the cause of failure of programs. We kept on it day after day, right on top of it, improved the system and we went along, made sure everybody was following the system and had a way of checking them out each time and evaluating them to see how well they were doing in meeting the requirements we set up.

After imposing these things, we set up a series of evaluations at the contractor's plant. We sent our teams into the contractor's plants to see how he's doing, to see how he's managing his program, what he's doing, how he's training his people—all those things that we felt were necessary—how he's carrying out his inspections, what was the inspection, was he paying attention to the documentation or just doing it out of his head. All these things were necessary to get a good tight program and know what you're doing, you see. Those things are in effect today. When we run these evaluations, I have a group, primarily Fleet Analysis Group Corona, California. (It used to be NOL Corona). I got them involved in the program.

We set these evaluations teams up, and they helped us in improving the documentation requirements, they helped us keep a tab on it, they helped us run these evaluations in the contracting plants, and it's a very worthwhile team. Just like we got

Vitro involved in coordination efforts, we've got FLTAC in the quality control and reliability programs to help us keep tabs on that. We've applied this across the board, across the board to everybody, and although we've done it in the early A-1 program, each time we rewrite these documents and improve this system with everybody's help. We're not doing this in a vacuum; we were getting all the contractors and everybody involved in it, all our field reps to help us make sure that we were doing it better and had a way of getting acceptance all the way across the board. A lot of people don't like for you to do this. You get to breathing down their neck too close.

John T. Mason, Jr.: Yes.

Mr. Buescher: But we find it keeps them on their toes. I feel SP field activities really don't like for us to do this, because they feel that's their job to make sure that the contractor does it. I disagree. We, SP, has a responsibility, and we're going to go in there and look at it and tell the SP field activity, "You're part of the team, so you come with us and help us evaluate it and then you follow up to make sure the contractor takes corrective action when we find something wrong." It works well and keeps everybody involved. When we report back, everybody in SP knows what we've found.

Sometimes we don't really find anything significant; sometimes we find some very significant things. Sometimes we find there have been changes in management in a company, changes in management attitude towards quality. Sometimes, quite often, we find that we have to go back and get a contractor reorganized and get the objectives squared away so that they're doing what we want them to do, and it's not an easy thing. You just keep at it, keep pounding on them, pounding on them, pounding on them. We require corrective action on anything we find, and we go back to reevaluate the corrective action.

The SP branch is part of this. We're not doing this as an overall group that's just coming in and kicking people around. Again, this was the thing that the branches didn't want us to do, and this was the thing that the contractors didn't want us to do, but now the branch is just great, and they go out with us, and they're part of the team. It varies between the branches. Some of them were absolutely great, because this is a tool for him to do his job. The branches are responsible for quality control, but on a system level we are.

John T. Mason, Jr.: Nothing succeeds like success.

Mr. Buescher: That's right. And when the problem was found, when we do the evaluations, before this group leaves the plant, they have a session to go over all these deficiencies that they've found and explain it and explain what has to be done. Then it's followed up with corrective action directed from SP to tell them to do it. We bring in whatever level of management is necessary. It may be the top guy or it may not; it depends on what we've found. They hear it and they understand it, and they ask questions before we leave.

John T. Mason, Jr.: You made some reference to the people in DoD being interested in how you did things. How close a touch did they maintain?

Mr. Buescher: More at an interference level in trying to make us not do things we were doing that we felt were necessary, more destructive than constructive.

John T. Mason, Jr.: That was probably because of lack of appreciation of your approach to things?

Mr. Buescher: No, some of these guys had worked with industry to come up with these standard specifications. Over the years, the Air Force was using them and the Army was using them. Why can't SP? We didn't think they were good enough, that's all. We did not think they were good enough; we didn't think that the inspection worked. We had to watch them. We weren't going to delegate things to them. If something was wrong, we were going to go out and find out about it, and we were going to get them squared away too.

This inspection service has been under many people many times, and it's changed. Sometimes they do a good job for you, and sometimes they don't. But they're not going to do a good job for you if they don't know you're watching them, I'll tell you that. In some places our field activities are just technical groups. In some cases, they are the contractor reps and they have the full function—not just technical function, but they have the contracting function and the inspection function. It's a big program and you have to keep on top of it. The only way we could do it is to get our program, ourselves involved and make sure people were meeting our requirements.

John T. Mason, Jr.: You did have some problem with DoD, did you not, when McNamara was there in terms of cost analysis?[*]

Mr. Buescher: Yes, but we didn't really have any problem. We ran cost analysis if it was necessary, and I think we met the objectives and pretty much did all right. SP has always had a very excellent measurement system in the area of finances and cost analysis and things of this sort. We didn't do it just the way everybody did it, but we were there first, you see. We did have a handle on our budget, and we have in almost every case come in within budget or slightly increased.

John T. Mason, Jr.: That was a protective guarantee, wasn't it?

Mr. Buescher: It helps. People had confidence in what we told them. That wasn't my area at all, but SP has always been able to respond and respond very rapidly to any request of this sort and come up with good answers and credible answers. I think that has been a very fine mark on our record, I'll tell you.

I'm going to tell you about the relationship with the fleet and the feedback. None of these things work if you don't get with the user and know what's happening in the fleet. Too often the fleet becomes sort of like orphans out there, doing the best they can. Nobody's really paying any attention to them, and there's no way for them to get the word back.

Starting with the first, we were very close with the fleet during shipbuilding time. This ship leaves the shipyard. And by the way, I want to tell you that all our ships leave the shipyard, go to Cape Canaveral, where they further train the crews, and they fire

---

[*] Robert S. McNamara served as Secretary of Defense from 21 January 1961 to 29 February 1968. His tenure was noted for his strong emphasis on cost-effectiveness.

missiles.* There has not been a single ship that was not ready to do that when it got down to the Cape to do the job. There never was a scheduled delay because of the weapon system not being on the line, and in the shipbuilding program there never was a delay in firing at the Cape. It always went down and was ready to go, ready to launch missiles. I think that's a real feather in our hat, and what I'm telling you is all the things that lead up to it. The programs that don't have the disciplines are going to have problems, like Eli Reich was telling you and I was telling you. You take the ship after completion and either send it to another shipyard for two or three years and try to make it work, or you just send it out and hope to God that somebody's going to get the weapon system working.

John T. Mason, Jr.: The more traditional shakedown cruise and then going back to the yard again because there were some bugs.

Mr. Buescher: Yes, but that's not the way to do it, and it doesn't have to be that way. I can never understand why we couldn't get other people outside the FBM program to pick up many of the things we did, but try as we can, we have not really convinced the Navy, the other parts of the Navy. Some of them are not able to do it because they're not organized to do it. The division of responsibility is such that somebody can't carry it through. We were organized to carry it all the way through to complete the job. Other people are not. They do a little piece and then turn it over to somebody else, and they do a little piece. You are losing things every time you switch this responsibility.

John T. Mason, Jr.: Now the SP project is much closer to the Navy as a whole, is it not, than it was originally under Raborn when it was a special project.

Mr. Buescher: Originally it was a project in the Navy and reported directly to the Secretary and to CNO. It is not a project under the Chief of Naval Material.

John T. Mason, Jr.: Yes, yes, that's what I mean. It changed status so it's closer, you would think, and the success of it would be more apparent.

---

* Cape Canaveral, Florida, is the site of missile firing by the National Aeronautics and Space Administration.

Mr. Buescher: It's very mystifying to me that people would come around all the time and say, "How do you do it? How do you keep these things on the line? You have such a good record." I go through this same thing I'm telling you, and the other people in SP also explain things in detail, and give them all the details and say we'd help them any way we can. Then they go away, and that's the end of it. Sometimes they try; sometimes it's too big to handle within the organization.

There are a lot of reasons that SP has done it, but that doesn't mean that everybody else can apply it, you see. Sometimes it will require a real reorganization. It requires a change in attitude towards budgets and where they allocate money. It required a permanency of people who were willing to stay with it. I stayed and had 25 years, system after system after system. Look how long Bob Wertheim was in. A lot of people who had been in SP were in there longer than I was. All of our branch engineers, two of them who had been there longer than I, retired before me. So it gives you an idea of the program.

John T. Mason, Jr.: It seems to me to be a source of great strength.

Mr. Buescher: It is a source of great strength, and you get a consistency that way so you don't have to start all over every time a new guy comes in and train him. The military has a change-over, and we have had a certain amount of change-over at the lower levels—technical as well as other levels—but SP and its policies and its discipline and its way of doing business, once established, have not changed over 25 years. It has been consistent.

John T. Mason, Jr.: Of course for the military, for the naval personnel, it sometimes has meant foregoing advancement to the top, hasn't it? Take Bob, for instance. He became an EDO, and so he was limited to the possibility of becoming a rear admiral.

Mr. Buescher: That's right, because there's no vice admiral EDO ordnance.

John T. Mason, Jr.: No.

Mr. Buescher: Look at Levering Smith. It took a special selection by President Kennedy to make him a rear admiral even.* He was passed over because—

John T. Mason, Jr.: He didn't conform to the pattern.

Mr. Buescher: That's right. He didn't conform to the pattern, but Kennedy promoted him.

John T. Mason, Jr.: So it calls for a special kind of dedication to the job, to the unit.

Mr. Buescher: It does. We have had people who've stayed with us years and years. Take Glen Clark, who's director now. I don't know how many years he's been in SP; he's been involved in our launcher branch, in our missile branch, fire control and guidance branch. He was technical director, and now he's director. He's come right up through the organization,

John T. Mason, Jr.: It's a source of great strength, and I can see it as a weakness, too, in that it's a small organization, and you don't have many men who have been through the ranks and then eventually are capable of becoming director. It's pretty limited. If something happened to one of them, then what?

Mr. Buescher: There was only one person from the outside who became director of the project. Of course, Raborn, and then Galantin came from the operational side and then Levering.†

John T. Mason, Jr.: But since that time it's all been—

Mr. Buescher: Bob Gooding, Bob Wertheim, and then Glen Clark have come up through

---

* John F. Kennedy served as President of the United States from 20 January 1960 until he was assassinated on 22 November 1963.
† Rear Admiral Ignatius J. Galantin, USN, served as director of the Special Projects Office from 26 February 1962 to 16 February 1965. In World War II he had been successful as commanding officer in diesel submarines. He covered the fleet ballistic missile program in some detail in his memoir Submarine Admiral (Urbana, University of Illinois Press, 1995).

the organization. It is kind of hard to find people now, I'll tell you, who have been so dedicated and who have this type of background and experience.

John T. Mason, Jr.: That's what I mean. And I suppose the possibility of going off into industry and the fabulous salaries is always a temptation. How is this sense of loyalty developed? This is an intangible thing, but how is it? Can you put words to it?

Mr. Buescher: One thing about SP—and I don't know if this is the answer—is that you can see things happening, you can become involved, you can see the results, you can implement it. Too many organizations don't have that; it's just doing something and you're doing a little piece of it. In SP things happen, and when the program gets started you know we've set up, depending on a lot of things such as the money and the need, we've set a date and we meet the date and you can be part of making that thing happen. You can stay with it. That's a source of satisfaction for all of us, you know, to have that feeling that you're a part of this team that has done this thing. And we've done it five times and getting ready to do it the sixth time.

John T. Mason, Jr.: So it's a family, really.

Mr. Buescher: It is a family, and they're all working together as a team. You have teamwork throughout the whole family.

John T. Mason, Jr.: Going back to what you were saying before about being mystified that the success of this system hasn't been copied elsewhere in the Navy, I had this observation to add. Most often, the CNO has been a fleet commander. Therefore, he must have been very much aware of the perfection of the unit you sent out, and it should have made its impression upon him at that point.

Mr. Buescher: "SP had all the money in the world and they could do anything they wanted to do." They explained it that way. That's a lot of bullshit, you know, frankly. It takes a lot more than that to do the job and do it right. That's not the answer.

As far as I know, the only comparable area in the Navy which has similar disciplines and similar controls is the nuclear power plant under Rickover. We seem to be the only two projects that have these types of controls.

John T. Mason, Jr.: And that has demonstrated the same kind of record.

Mr. Buescher: Yes, yes, same kind of record.

John T. Mason, Jr.: But it also has been subjected to a lot of flak because it's dealing with human beings in a larger sense than perhaps yours is.

Mr. Buescher: Well, I think Rickover himself has gotten involved in human control. We don't do that. We don't try to select commanding officers of the ships, we don't try to set up their training and things of this sort. SP does have a training branch, and we are now working through the Chief of Naval Training. We are responsible for that part of the training curriculum.

John T. Mason, Jr.: That's interesting. Tell me about it.

Mr. Buescher: All the weapons officers go through, and all the people that get involved in the weapons system go through that training. SP is responsible for the design and construction of the buildings that go into a complex training site. We're responsible with the Chief of Naval Training to make sure they get the right curriculum and the facilities are designed and constructed.

John T. Mason, Jr.: Where is this located?

Mr. Buescher: We have a number of training facilities. We had one in New London, we had one in Charleston, in Pearl Harbor, all the home ports. We have a brand-new one out at our Trident facility on the West Coast near Seattle where the Navy will refit the new

Trident SSBNs that were coming out.* It's a very necessary thing.

John T. Mason, Jr.: What personnel really are trained there?

Mr. Buescher: Naval personnel, crews of the Trident SSBN that go out on patrols.

John T. Mason, Jr.: How does that job with Rickover's training program in Connecticut?

Mr. Buescher: I'm talking about the weapon system.

John T. Mason, Jr.: Oh, I see.

Mr. Buescher: He has his own training program. He also has an authority in the selection of commanding officers and officers and crew that go to make up that part of the ship that has to do with the power plant. He doesn't have anything to do with the selection of the weapons people. That's not his area. The commanding officer, the exec, the engineering officer and anybody that's going to get their hands into ship's propulsion he controls. They all have to have an interview with him after going through a selection process. SP doesn't get involved in that, and that's a very controversial area.† You'll find a lot of comments about Rickover in that area. But that's not our area. Our area is to try to get these guys trained to do our weapon system job.

John T. Mason, Jr.: That's where I referred to the flak because that has produced flak.

Mr. Buescher: It does produce flak any time you are controlling things to the extent he is controlling it. It will produce a lot of comment.

---

* For a description of the SSBN base at Bangor, Washington, see Jim Davis, "Building the Tridents' Home," U.S. Naval Institute Proceedings, March 1979, pages 62-73. The East Coast counterpart is a Kings Bay, Georgia.
† The controversy ended in March 1982, shortly after this interview, when Admiral Kinnaird R. McKee, USN, succeeded Admiral Rickover as Director of the Naval Nuclear Propulsion Program.

John T. Mason, Jr.: These schools are scattered around in various places. What central control is maintained by your people over them?

Mr. Buescher: They are scattered about because they are where the off-duty crew is—the two-crew concept. They are home-ported where their families are so that in the period that they're not at sea, you give them refresher training, you see. That has to do with location of the weapon system trainers.

We watch it very carefully. We have one branch that has a full-time job in SP, to worry about the training function and to work with the Chief of Naval Personnel and the Chief of Naval Training to make sure we are keeping up the quality of the people that we are getting, that they are all getting the right kind of training, anything of this sort. They are right in there with it to provide, buy, and install the right equipments for which they are trained. They buy from the rest of the branches the operational equipments that go in a submarine. They put them in the trainers, come up with a curriculum of the best way to train these crews, keep tabs on the guys and what they're doing and how well they're doing. So it's more of a technical function rather than trying to keep all those people—

John T. Mason, Jr.: And what's the retention rate in that area?

Mr. Buescher: I don't remember the number. But they keep tabs on that, and some years you have bad years and you don't have a very good rate. Some years it's pretty good, particularly when they started giving them reenlistment bonuses and things of this sort.

John T. Mason, Jr.: Amazing bonuses. Does a man have a refresher course after every tour?

Mr. Buescher: They get training after every tour. That's part of their in-patrol thing. If problems came up that maybe they hadn't been able to handle, or they didn't quite understand or there had been changes to the system, those SP-alts that were put in, the changes in documentation, maybe something came up and they wanted to review all that trouble and failure report—I was going to tell you about that.

We had an excellent trouble and failure reporting system that we managed centrally through my staff. They worked with the branches and the contractors to get these things out and followed up on them to make sure corrective action was taken where needed. You don't try to correct everything that happens just because somebody said it didn't work. We try to get a trend and see if it's happened more than once or if it's something we ought to spend time and effort and money on.

John T. Mason, Jr.: There's no gullibility there?

Mr. Buescher: No. This is a very excellent program. So many of these type feedback programs are built and managed such that the fleet puts in information into a big black pit, and that's the last you ever hear of it. We have teams that go out and meet the crews in an off-period time, to work with them on the trouble and failure reporting systems and the problem that they'd had and try to explain to them what's happening when we had answers, to try to help them correct their procedures to do it better. It's a very close relationship we have with the fleet. They respond, they really do. Those fleet guys think we've taken care of them, they send in TFR reports and tell us everything, whether it's maybe an equipment problem or a procedure problem or maybe a document that's written wrong and tells them how to operate the equipment.[*] It may be a maintenance procedure. It may be a lack of something in the spare parts program that we have that's supporting them. Anything that they want to put on the TFR, we take it and we do something with that. We read it, we understand it and, if necessary, we take action.

John T. Mason, Jr.: That automatically eliminates a sense of frustration.

Mr. Buescher: Yes, it does because you're not going to get a response from these guys if you don't do something to let them know you're thinking about them and trying to take care of them.

John T. Mason, Jr.: That should help in reenlistment and all the rest of it, then.

---

[*] TFR—trouble and failure report.

Mr. Buescher: It gives them a better feeling that what they're doing is important. That's really the key.

John T. Mason, Jr.: And it eliminates the gripes. Does SP get concerned about boredom on those long tours of duty at sea? Is that one of their concerns too?

Mr. Buescher: We're concerned with it but only with our training system, working primarily with the Chief of Naval Training and the BuPers, do we get involved in that in coming up and recommending courses sometimes. It may be college courses with credit that they're able to take or exercise equipment—all these kinds of things that would fill in their time properly, not just to make work for them. We don't want to maintain our system just to keep busy. We want to keep their hands off of it unless the equipment needs it, you see. They go through all kinds of drills and what they call weapon system readiness trial, WSRT.

When a message comes out, they don't know if it's the real thing or not or whether they're going to fire a missile. They go through a countdown. We have instrumentation aboard the ship that follows that right down, and if a part of a subsystem doesn't work, that's all recorded. We know where it is, and we're able to get APL involved in this, and we're able to keep records on a daily basis and on a yearly basis and a whole time operational time from boat to boat, on the reliability of the system, the subsystem and pieces of equipment. All that is fed back to the fleet so they know what they're doing and who's doing things wrong. It's quite a good relationship, and by having our fingers on this thing, it's paid off handsomely.

John T. Mason, Jr.: I would think so. SP must have had some hand in the design of the crew quarters, then, on ships and the facilities for them there.

Mr. Buescher: To some extent we have. That's primarily the NavSea end of it, not ours. Through our branch, SP 26, we establish our requirements, whatever they may be—crews or the number of people—and we help where we can, but it's not primarily our job to do that.

John T. Mason, Jr.: But you certainly are cognizant of it as part of the whole picture,

Mr. Buescher: As a matter of fact, even in Raborn's days, we were giving them exercise equipment, bicycles and weightlifting equipment and all that.

John T. Mason, Jr.: I'm sure he went in for that.

Mr. Buescher: We didn't know what they needed, but these are good things to have. The commanding officer, during the shipbuilding program, would come in and say, "I have to have this and that." And we'd find money for them and buy it and put it aboard for them, you see. It's a little more formal now these days than it was then. It's all part of getting the job done.

John T. Mason, Jr.: There's more to say, is there not, about checking on the failures and so forth that you were going to talk about?

Mr. Buescher: I told you about the trouble with the failure reporting system and our follow-up and our fleet's follow-up. It's just a very good system. Nobody else in the Navy has one like it. We do not use anybody else's system. Other systems, other bureaus, other activities have trouble, they have a common system. They've standardized it now, the whole NavSea; everybody uses the same thing. But, frankly, that system stinks. It's not new; I've said this many times. All the data goes back, all the feedback does not go into some activity and it's lost. I don't mean many activities; it goes into a single activity who's supposed to do something with them. Ours goes back to the branches, the subcontractor and the guy in the subsystem contract who can do something about it, you see. We've got people full time following these systems and keeping their fingers on them, on the problems coming up and how to correct them. He can't change a design unless he comes back through the SP-alt system again, but he can make a proposal. All these guys are set up to follow through on this thing and provide this long-term support. They are very sensitive to this thing and what's happening out there, and with our branches they set up meetings with the fleet and go out and talk it over. They are very conscientious about this whole thing.

John T. Mason, Jr.: It sounds like a tremendous master plan that has been developed and the wisdom in the development—

Mr. Buescher: As I said, we had a free hand to do it. That helped.

John T. Mason, Jr.: And you had a small organization.

Mr. Buescher: They didn't have to come out as well as they did, but it did come out, and we were free to do it the way we wanted to do it. Too many programs—I won't say what program it was, but there was a new project manager organization set up a few years ago, handling brand-new missile systems. Everything was done to make our experience available, and many people tried to get them to do it this way. They wouldn't have anything to do with it. They've got troubles ahead, you watch. They've got troubles ahead, because they have not paid attention to this kind of detail.

John T. Mason, Jr.: I remember Eli telling me that when he was made so-called czar of the 3-T program, people like Freddie Withington and others insisted that it should be another SP project. He resisted this like mad all along and said it couldn't be another SP project, because it was already under way, and there were all these components in existence, and it just wouldn't work.

Mr. Buescher: You'd have to change a lot of things to make it work.

John T. Mason, Jr.: Yes. There were too many people involved in it already when he took over.

Mr. Buescher: Doing it the conventional way.

John T. Mason, Jr.: Yes.

Mr. Buescher: On many occasions, it's not worth a damn.

John T. Mason, Jr.: Really, it is something that has to start from scratch.

Mr. Buescher: They've had opportunities where they did not do it. As a matter of fact, they deliberately did not do it, and they've got problems ahead. You can see it coming. Big project too.

John T. Mason, Jr.: One can almost say knowingly wouldn't it be great if we had an SP project for our federal government?

Mr. Buescher: What I've really been stressing is we have developed—the management of the project—we've developed a sense of long-time control and direction. We've set up disciplines and systems of organization for applying these disciplines in a uniform manner throughout the systems. We all do it one way. We don't let a subsystem or a contractor do it differently.

John T. Mason, Jr.: And you might add, I suppose, with almost the same personnel involved all along doing it.

Mr. Buescher: That's right. We have gotten control and decision at the system level rather than separately by each subsystem in many of these things, just that way to make it come up for decision. And we provided a technical overview and control at the system level. That's very important. What this has done is given SP a consistent and uniform way of doing business, not just in the technical area, but in the budgeting area and in its planning and everything else. This has provided a consistent basis in which these things can be done. It's helped the management of the project.

I think that we've talked about the consistency of people and how they stayed with us. It's been a fun program, a real fun program. Hard, long hours, but one in which you get a lot of satisfaction out of it, and it's a lot of fun. Sometimes it gets kind of loud and noisy and people are beating on each other and the blood flows. Our systems are designed for production. They're designed for maintenance and operation in the fleet by the submarine people in that environment. I think that's what it all adds up to.

John T. Mason, Jr.: Was there any noticeable change in the whole atmosphere when Raborn retired from the project, he being so essentially an out-front man?

Mr. Buescher: Of course, as an individual, we missed him and we missed his ability to work with Congress, to work with the President or whoever had to give acceptance for this thing and the way we were doing business. Galantin came along, and he wasn't there long enough. He and Raborn both had Smith behind them, you see, and that kept going on, the technical division did not change. We missed him. Other than our interface with the outside world and politics, Levering Smith is a pretty smart guy.

John T. Mason, Jr.: He's a very quiet fellow, though.

Mr. Buescher: Very quiet, but he's very effective too.

John T. Mason, Jr.: Is he ably effective with Congress?

Mr. Buescher: I don't think anybody's as effective with Congress as Raborn was. Raborn had a knack, I'll tell you that. He was a real PR man.

John T. Mason, Jr.: Yes, that was one of his predominant traits.

Mr. Buescher: That's right.

John T. Mason, Jr.: He talked about going out into the factories and getting the wives there and talking about the urgency of this whole thing.

John B. Buescher, Interview #2 (1/28/82) -- Page 106

Mr. Buescher: We'd have meetings and invite all the families to SP, you know.

John T. Mason, Jr.: That certainly is a PR effort.

Mr. Buescher: One thing I wanted to tell you about was the U.K. program.

John T. Mason, Jr.: Oh, yes. I want to hear about that.

Mr. Buescher: I was deeply involved in that.

John T. Mason, Jr.: You and Bob both.

Mr. Buescher: Yes. We took the lead in organizing the management of that program. They came in, and they were scared of us because we had done all these great things. They didn't know how to interface with us; they didn't know how this thing was going to go. In too many programs with foreign governments, we sell them the equipments and then forget them; they're on their own to keep it up. They get all of the changes, but then it's up to them to keep them and follow through. That's a mistake if you're really interested in that system and has also been a deterrent in part of our system. There has to be some way to keep them together.

    When they first came aboard, I personally wrote a whole series of documents we called technical arrangements which spelled out how this program was to be managed, what we were going to do for them—not only to get them to agree to it, but also to tell our people what their responsibility was in helping support that program. It was a book about this thick of separate technical arrangements.

John T. Mason, Jr.: About five inches thick.

Mr. Buescher: It went into every area, each of these areas we've talked about. We do their configuration control; they didn't take that over. We treat them just like one of our boats, and we give them hell when they try to step out of line, just like we do one of our branches.

John T. Mason, Jr.: They accepted that without question?

Mr. Buescher: They had a choice. I gave them a choice. It finally got it down to the point where their pride was hurting, and I went over there and I met with the top guys over there and I told them, "You do it this way, or we write it this way and you've got it. There's not going to be any doubt about who's got the responsibility, because this thing is either going to go or not going to go, and we're going to know who's going to be responsible." So they agreed to our disciplines and control. Everything we do for our system we do for theirs. When we put in an SP-alt, when we put in a change in documentation, the arrangement was that they would have money here so we could automatically order a SP-alt kit or a new set of documentation and distribute it to them. We didn't have to go ask them. We did it absolutely automatically just like for our system. They had a pot of money here we could draw on. That was very important, because for every little decision the money guys wanted to get in and price it out and do other things. But we got it so it was automatic. The technical guys over there wanted it that way, and I pushed it.

John T. Mason, Jr.: How unique to achieve that.

Mr. Buescher: It is unique. It is unique.

John T. Mason, Jr.: Will that pertain also with the Trident system they take on?

Mr. Buescher: If they take it on, it will apply. I just went through that whole thing before I retired and redid that whole technical arrangement to make it apply to the Trident system, just the same way. Their boats, their firings of missiles at the Cape—we consider that part of our operation, because anything we do for our boats, they do for theirs. Everything we do for our weapon system, they do for their weapon system.

John T. Mason, Jr.: What about their crews? Are they trained in your schools?

Mr. Buescher: They have their own schools, but they use our curriculum with changes somewhat to fit their language and fit their way of doing things. Yes, we helped them build their school over there and gave them our curriculum for weapon systems.

John T. Mason, Jr.: So it pays off in terms of they are a part of our defense system.

Mr. Buescher: We consider them part of our system. They don't have many boats; they only have four. That's four more, you know. They operate the way they want to at sea and go to their launch areas and things of this sort, but they agreed to make every change we made in our system; automatically they have to accept it. Many times they don't want to do it and we say, "Oh no, you agreed to it," and they make the changes. "Here's the kit; we've already bought it for you."

John T. Mason, Jr.: I can see where that is very difficult.

Mr. Buescher: It's difficult particularly for the follow-on people to accept. From time to time people have come into the program who want to change it; they want to just kind of change it. But we won't let them. You either change it all the way. You can't be halfway pregnant, you see. Somebody's got to take the responsibility, and that's what this is all about—who's responsible for keeping it up. We also find from time to time our branches have a tendency, some of them, to kind of back off and not want to support the U.K. because they've got so much work in the U.S. program. They don't want to do it to the same degree. Then we hit them over the head with a U.S.-U.K. agreement that said that's our U.S. responsibility. Let's keep on. Let's do this job right. So these technical arrangements have served very effectively to control that program.

John T. Mason, Jr.: It had a rocky beginning, did it not, because I understand they were terribly let down in terms of this other project they were interested in. What was it called, the Skybolt or something?*

Mr. Buescher: Yes, I believe that was it and thus cancelled it.

John T. Mason, Jr.: And we cancelled it because it didn't meet our needs any longer, and they were left high and dry. It must have been rocky going at the time.

Mr. Buescher: It wasn't long because at the same time they cancelled it, Kennedy—they met in Bermuda, you know. Kennedy offered to them our Polaris system. We got a whole lot of material ready for that group, that mission that went down there with Kennedy so they could make this offer. The Royal Navy thought it was great because that Skybolt was an Air Force project, you see. They brought the Royal Navy into the whole picture, and they thought that was just the greatest thing in the world.[†]

---

* Skybolt was canceled in December 1962. It involved a ballistic missile, armed with a nuclear warhead and designed for a range of approximately 1,000 miles, to be fired from planes such as the B-52 bomber.

† For an insider's account of the U.S.-U.K. Polaris program, see I. J. Galantin, "The Resolution of Polaris," U.S. Naval Institute Proceedings, April 1985, pages 80-88.

John B. Buescher, Interview #3 (3/4/82) -- Page 110

Interview Number 3 with Mr. John B. Buescher

Place: Mr. Buescher's residence in Falls Church, Virginia

Date: Thursday, 4 March 1982

Interviewer: John T. Mason, Jr.

John T. Mason, Jr.: Well, sir, I've been looking forward to this number three of your very interesting series. Incidentally, that last interview I thought was fascinating on the organizational nature of the SP project. Do you want to pick up the story at this point and perhaps talk about—in an unclassified way—the Polaris and the Poseidon and the evolvement of the missiles?

Mr. Buescher: As you know, early in the program, when the Navy first got in on the program of putting a ballistic missile on a ship—

John T. Mason, Jr.: We first began to deal with this in the year 1955.

Mr. Buescher: Yes, 1955. The first thing they did, of course, was to organize the project within the Navy to handle it. That's when they brought Raborn in and set him up as the project manager. At that time, the project was to marry the Jupiter missile, the Army missile, with a submarine and take that liquid propellant missile to sea in a submarine.[*] The Navy got going real fast on this, but it was obvious that there were a lot of serious problems with carrying liquids, particularly on a submarine, safety being one.

John T. Mason, Jr.: One gets the idea that the Navy was a little bit appalled at this idea.

Mr. Buescher: I don't think they had really looked at it very carefully, and the more they

---

[*] The Jupiter intermediate-range ballistic missile ballistic missile was developed by the Army at Redstone Arsenal in Alabama under the direction of Dr. Wernher von Braun. However, in 1956 the Department of Defense limited the Army's operational employment of missiles to those with less than a 200-mile range. Thus when Jupiter became operational in 1959 it was under U.S. Air Force control.

got into it, the more they began to see that this was a little monster. There was nothing wrong with the Jupiter, but the Jupiter in a submarine is quite something. I think there were several reasons for it. First and foremost was the safety. Carrying liquid propellants in a submarine is a danger, and the possibility of leaks could kill all of the people in the submarine or cause an explosion. Not only an explosion, but breathing the fumes of this propellant can kill you; they're highly toxic. Secondly, lift-off of a liquid propellant, when you fire the rocket and you launch it, lift-off is extremely slow as it builds up velocity. On a solid propellant, lift-off is very fast. It's not hard to see a situation, to take a calculated situation in which you can't launch the liquid-propellant missile from a seagoing platform. In rough weather the ship will roll, pitch, yaw, heave, and the acceleration forces may be such to cause the missile with such a slow lift-off and low velocity to topple and come back on the submarine.

John T. Mason, Jr.: Wasn't the size a factor also?

Mr. Buescher: Another factor was the size; because of being a liquid-propellant rocket, it takes a lot more room to contain the propellant.* In addition, the Jupiter carried a much heavier warhead than Polaris, for approximately the same damage capability. The missile itself was just too big, and you can only get a very few aboard a submarine. Whether it's a liquid or a solid propellant, the Navy felt that it could design a missile to meet its requirement in a much more compact size.

John T. Mason, Jr.: Do you recall the circumference of the Jupiter?

Mr. Buescher: I have it, if it's important. But I've forgotten what it is. They were using a front-end nuclear warhead based on a technology which the Navy found through the AEC, which was much too large for what they could do at the time.†

---

* The first version of the submarine-launched Polaris ballistic missile, the A-1, was 28 feet long, 4 feet in diameter, and weighed about 30,000 pounds. It had a range of 1,200 nautical miles. The A-2 version was 31 feet long; 4 feet, 6 inches in diameter; and weighed about 30,000 pounds. It had a range of 1,725 nautical miles. The A-3 version was 32 feet long; 4 feet, 6 inches in diameter; and weighed about 35,000 pounds. It had a range of 2,880 nautical miles.
† AEC—Atomic Energy Commission.

If you based a development at that time—Dr. Teller was the one who told the Navy, "You're doing it wrong. The AEC has come along so far with the new developments in the warhead technology that the AEC could give us a warhead much, much smaller in size and much less in weight than was on board the Jupiter and could do the same job." That helped bring the size of the missile down considerably, and it didn't need near as much thrust to carry it.[*]

John T. Mason, Jr.: Those remarks were the famous remarks of Teller at Woods Hole, were they not?

Mr. Buescher: I believe so. At this point in time, I hadn't really joined the project. I was involved because the solid-propellant technology of the Navy was in my branch in BuOrd, and it was our people, along with Levering Smith, who were feeding all of this information into the Navy group to help them make this decision. It was at the time that the Navy in late September of 1956 had set up a project with DoD approval, SecDef approval, to go ahead and look into and develop a solid propellant and do away with the Jupiter because of some of the problems I just told you about. It was in late December of 1956 that I joined the project. I had a lot of background, and I was on the edge of this decision the whole time, being part of the group of providing information to the Navy group to help them come to that decision.

After a decision for the Navy to proceed, the Navy Special Projects then went through a study period to determine what they could do in terms of weapon system characteristics, missile range, submarine size, number of missiles, etc. A whole series of tradeoff studies was undertaken to try to put it together as to a total weapon system, using the steering task group as the platform to present all of these trade-off studies. The steering task group was made up of not only SP and government activities but all of the top most capable people at its contractors.

SSPO had brought aboard a whole group of contractors who have stayed with the

---

[*] Dr. Edward Teller, a highly respected Hungarian-born physicist, was the prime mover in the creation of the U.S. hydrogen bomb, which was first detonated in 1952. For details on the beginning of the program, see William F. Whitmore, "The Origin of Polaris," U.S. Naval Institute Proceedings, March 1980, pages 55-59.

program for the last 25 years.* Out of all of that came a general concept of what the weapon would be and what the size of the submarine would be and how many missiles it could carry, the characteristics of the warhead, the range of the missile, missile guidance concepts, what kind of navigation system you had to install in the ship, and how to launch the missile. It was decided we would launch it using air pressure to push it out of the launch tube. It would then ignite, and then it would take off.

John T. Mason, Jr.: How long did it take all of this to gel?

Mr. Buescher: This went on for about three or four months. I was aboard when they had their first meeting; I got there just in time and participated in that. It was several months for this to get out of the way, and then we had to write a specifications system based on the general characteristics to get it down to a much more specific level so that each of the subsystems would know exactly what their job would be. I was given the task of running an accuracy study to try to prorate accuracy amongst the subsystems.

We may have talked about this the last time. If we had X number of nautical-mile-accuracy goal, you had to break that down so each subsystem in missile and guidance and navigation would know what their contribution would be, you see. We ran a study using our system contractors and involving the subsystems when we felt we had to. We prorated that accuracy contribution to keep it within. It also pointed out where redundancy in the system was necessary. For instance, if you had one piece of equipment in the navigation system, if it went down, then the whole system went down. In order to overcome this problem, then multiple installations of a particular piece of equipment were provided so that at least one of them would always be ready to use, depending on the reliability you expect out of that piece of equipment.

John T. Mason, Jr.: That was quite a strategic spot, wasn't it?

Mr. Buescher: Yes. For instance, we ended up putting three ship inertial navigational systems—the same one, three of a kind—aboard the ship because of this. The navigation

---

* SSPO—Strategic Systems Project Office, as it was known at the time of the interview.

subsystem gave us our north direction as a reference and gave us our speed over the ground. As a reference it gave this type of information that was very vital in order to establish a ballistics baseline for the weapon systems. The fire control took that information and provided ballistics and other data which was transmitted to guidance. There were other places in the system where we did, too, but that was the worst one. You find a lot of people who say it's crazy putting in three SINS, because they take so much room, but it paid off. It's very difficult to express in dollars what down time of a system means.

John T. Mason, Jr.: Down time?

Mr. Buescher: That's inoperability. For instance, if we had one SINS aboard, and it was down for 50 hours on a patrol, if you had to determine that in terms of what does it cost the nation in dollars, in readiness, it's quite a significant thing. You can't afford to do that. You develop these systems to have them ready, and you get them out on patrol and you expect them to be ready when needed. That was our goal from the very first: to have them ready all of the time, because we were working toward a full wartime goal and not a peacetime goal.

John T. Mason, Jr.: That was a rather brilliant idea, wasn't it, to incorporate that?

Mr. Buescher: I thought it was. It wasn't necessarily my idea, but I participated in it to help come up with this type of thing.

John T. Mason, Jr.: This was pioneering, wasn't it? This concept hadn't been used elsewhere, had it?

Mr. Buescher: I presume it must have. Our next stop then was not just in accuracy but in every area that was to involve the subsystems to come up with a statement of what requirements we were placing on them to which they had to develop their subsystems equipments. Essentially, we were trying to work to a point where we would give them requirements. We would tell them what they had to do and what we expected from them in terms of signals or in terms of outputs they had to generate. We wanted each subsystem to do its job without concern that other subsystems with which it interfaced might be doing things that affected them.

For instance, when other subsystems, although they—what we were saying to them is, "We at the system level are putting a fence around you. We're giving you our requirements and telling you what your output has to be and who you have to put out to, and we're telling you how many people you can have to operate the system, we're telling you what your readiness goals have to be, your readiness time, we're prorating reliability goals to you, we're saying what your reaction time has to be after the alert comes to get on the line." We were breaking it down pretty fine so that they could understand their job and we could measure them as to how well they were doing.

John T. Mason, Jr.: I think it might be well for the record to list the composition of this mastermind, I mean the individuals who served on this steering committee.

Mr. Buescher: You mean in pulling it together?

John T. Mason, Jr.: Yes.

Mr. Buescher: We first went through the series of studies using STG as a platform. I don't have the names of those people. The real technical boss of that was Levering Smith. We worked with all the SSPO branch personnel and contractors to come up with this scheme; we worked with CNO in the operational aspects; we worked with special advisors from government laboratories and industry. If there was somebody of particular knowledge in a particular area, we'd bring him in. We didn't stay in any bounds as to whom we would bring in and where we got our knowledge from. If knowledge was lacking, we got it so that we understood the problem.

John T. Mason, Jr.: In other words, it wasn't a fixed group.

Mr. Buescher: No, it wasn't a fixed group. It was run out of the technical director's office. Levering Smith and I put it together, using everybody we could and using all the STG workers who had the background as a framework for the whole thing. We had special contractors who reported just to us and helped us do it, and we went to the subsystem branches and the subsystem contractors when necessary. There wasn't any limit. We just took the job of pulling it all together and putting it out on a specification form, a goal in mind. Levering Smith and I did that. I'm not sure we're not repeating some of the stuff we talked of before, but that's such an important point, it doesn't hurt to repeat it.

John T. Mason, Jr.: You haven't repeated it in the sense that you've talked about it before.

Mr. Buescher: Most programs go at it quite differently. I've had experience where I have kind of watched from the side. They go at it quite differently, and they have gone at it in a way that's not very effective. This has been a very effective way, kind of keeping your fingers on things and setting it up and with everybody in the program understanding what's going on and what their job is and bringing the overall system and problems up to the system level for control. Again, that's what I was talking about the last time.

What we are trying to do is have a way of controlling the project and have a way of controlling it, so that we know not in every detail what is going on, but whenever there was a problem arising in a subsystem on a subsystem basis, we could highlight it and make sure it was brought forward. It's so easy when you run into problems to explain them away, to say, "I've got a little fix and I'll fix it." And then that fix doesn't work, and it goes on. Each little fix takes about three to six months to a year, and the first thing you know, you're in real trouble because you didn't really get on to solving the problem with both feet. That's when the problem grows.

It's typical of a thing that can happen to you if you let problems go along and let people explain those problems, saying, "Oh, all we have to do is make this little change," and, "All right, we accept that." And they go back and four or five months later it's something else, and then four or five months something else happens, and it goes on and on and on. You can get a whole development program in trouble that way if you don't have some way of highlighting these things and really putting the pressure on them when problems come up and bringing in anybody you need to help you solve these problems. That's what we were trying to do in organizing SSPO. We were trying to set up that program so that if there was a problem, everybody knows about it and secondly, if anybody needs help, we'll get it to them.

John T. Mason, Jr.: And I suppose by subdividing and establishing parameters for the various groups, you tended to prevent this.

Mr. Buescher: Yes, it gave us an effective way of managing the program. What I'm telling you now I told to many, many people outside of SP, and to many, many other projects in answers to people who come and say, "How does SP do it? Why do they have so much success and we have all of these problems?" To me this is an extremely important thing; it's the important thing in a project to be able to run it in the proper manner. These people come in and then when it's all over, after I've given them this whole speech, they end up saying, "Now, what do you [SP] really do? Tell us what you really do that's different."

They're not listening to what I'm telling them; it didn't get across. The difference in SP management from other projects must be so subtle that they don't catch it. A lot of people in SP don't catch it; it takes them a long time, but it's management technique that has proved extremely successful, and I feel very proud that I've been part of it to help come up with it. It's a very detailed thing and a lot of people don't like to work in detail, you see. But it's an extremely detailed thing, and it requires that you personally—and I'm not talking about not just me but the technical director too—do get involved in many, many details of the program. Many people in similar places in other programs think that's none of their business, that it's too detailed.

Levering Smith was very strong on signature authority in the mail—who could sign mail at SP and who could not sign mail in SP. You say, well, that's all detail; why can't we delegate this thing down? But you know who could sign mail in SP? The director (that was Wertheim), the deputy director, the director and deputy director of the planning and program division and three of us in the technical division—myself, the technical director and the deputy technical director. That's all of the people who could sign the mail going outside of SP.

In order to cut down on the amount of work—there was a tremendous amount of work in our spare parts material support area, like ship two of these gadgets here and ship six of these here. Of that little detail we gave signature authority to one of our staff sections. With anything on policy or anything that commits SP, it still had to come up for signature at the higher level. Signature authority was very strictly controlled. This is one other example of the type of detailed control SP branches got from the top.

We'd get letters from other Navy offices such as NavSea, Material, or NavElex signed about ten levels down with no coordination within the command originating.[*] Sometimes you'd get two letters on the same subject from a command, from different parts of it, which were entirely different. You didn't get that at SP. You got one story out of SP because it was felt to be important enough to control what was being said and what was being committed. It's a tedious job to be involved in that kind of control, but we did it. And that's one of the types of controls.

John T. Mason, Jr.: I suppose you did it because you were convinced of its effectiveness, so you did it willingly.

Mr. Buescher: You recognize why you do it. Some of it was strictly routine stuff, awfully routine. But some of it was very important, and there was no way of saying, "This is routine and you sign it our branch," or "This is important, you send it to us." Because people's attitudes and understandings change over a period of time, you have people coming and going and some of them are challenges, and they think they're going to recreate the world, but some of them are not. You'd be continually beating these people down if you did it any other way, so let it all come up. We always turned back a lot of mail that we didn't agree with. A branch would say, "Well, you gave me a job to do." That's right. "You gave me your requirement." That's right. "I've got a contract and you say to go ahead and get the job done and you'll give me the money to do it." That's right. "Then let me do my job." Your job is also to report to us, you see.

---

[*] NavElex—Naval Electronics Systems Command.

John T. Mason, Jr.: To keep that control.

Mr. Buescher: Yes. We kept beating this around because a lot of people, even after you told them, they didn't understand, or they think it's a lot of stuff, but it is a degree of control that you maintain and always maintain that I think has been just great—tedious but great.

John T. Mason, Jr.: Go on and say how all of this developed into Polaris itself.

Mr. Buescher: We got it to where we were giving everybody their requirement. In the meantime, they had all proceeded to get organized and get their development programs going, set up the reins so we could do our firings and all that. It was natural then to allocate the money, once you told them what the job was, to have the budget reviewed to allocate the money and give them the money so they could proceed and start working with the fleet, the operators, the boat operators, including CNO, on the operational aspects of it, which we did. It just followed naturally with a heck of a lot of hard work on everybody's part to get this thing going. As you go along, you come up with new ways of testing and new ways to better manage the program so that you can keep this thing under control. Where you find that maybe somebody has gotten off on the wrong track and they are coming to a blind alley on a development, we have to turn that thing around so that you get it in a more productive avenue.

John T. Mason, Jr.: Are there any major incidents of that sort that developed in this stage?

Mr. Buescher: Generally, the approaches to development had all been pretty well thought through with a lot of experience behind it. I think, for instance, this business—just take the launching, the method of launching the missile from the submarine. That was a new concept. A lot of people really thought we were overstepping technology to go that way, but it turned out to be pretty straightforward. Applying good engineering to it solved the problem. A lot of people had a lot of ideas on what they wanted to do, some of them kind of far out. We had to weed a lot of that out of the program and get it down to a practical approach.

John T. Mason, Jr.: A project of this sort would naturally inspire imagination in a very fertile mind, would it not?

Mr. Buescher: That's exactly right. And it took a lot of talking and a lot of thinking through to make sure everybody was proceeding on the same way of operating and maintaining the system. For instance, you'd find one guy who expected that if his subsystem went down while at sea on a 60-day patrol he would come up to the surface and fix it, because that's the way he could fix it from the outside the SSBN. Well, you have to beat that down. You can't do that; we're going out there for 60 days and not coming up.

Or you'd find somebody who was trying to develop a system and keep it maintained by letting the crew do a lot of fidgeting with the system and tweaking it and doing all this stuff, forgetting the fact that this guy's going to be on for 60 days and then another guy is going to take that place in 60 days and go back out to sea. You have to have a system that's maintainable under those particular conditions. We were constantly putting that down and keeping that type of thing from happening, to keep everybody on the same track in that respect. Where necessary, we did run parallel developments of the same item where it looked like one of them was of a high risk (where if you got it you'd really have something) and then in some of those areas we had come up with a less-of-a-risk development and we'd run it in parallel. You'd run it up to a point to where you don't do it all the way through; you do it to a point where you can see whether or not you're going to make it with the high risk one and if you do, then you cancel one, the less-of-a-risk one and go on with that.

Communications, although not directly SP's problem, was something nobody was doing anything about, it was some other bureau's job and SP got involved with it. One of the things they looked at was a wire-guided torpedo in the Navy.

John T. Mason, Jr.: A wire-guided one, yes.

Mr. Buescher: Maybe Eli told you about that. The wire stayed hooked to the fire control in the boat always, and it would go out. It was always a trailing wire, you see, and they could give it guidance and things of this sort. Well, one of the kind of far-out things that we looked at—Raborn was pushing it—was a wire-guided communications system that would always be hooked up by a link to the shore. You can imagine after so many patrols you had the whole bottom of the ocean covered with copper wire. You'd say, "Well, we'll just reel it in." But it would break, it was just going to break a lot of times, you see. That's one of the things we looked at. You know, it helps stimulate the mind. Whether you thought it was going to be practical or not didn't make any difference; we didn't spend a lot of money, but it did help to stimulate people into doing something and feel they had to solve that problem.

John T. Mason, Jr.: It makes it pretty vulnerable.

Mr. Buescher: Particularly in the navigation system. That was where we were pushing the state of the art considerably beyond what had been experienced before. The subsystem contractor and our branch came up with a lot of things that helped focus on the problem that you knew, but you knew you weren't ever going to use some of this stuff. You couldn't use it because it made the operation of the submarine too difficult. I don't mean just the steering of it, but I mean the communications back and forth, and I mean the whole concept of operations.

In the launching, for example, we had a number of ways of pushing that missile out of the submarine, and we finally settled on use of air pressure, and in later systems we came up with something different. We used a hot gas to push it out. That hadn't been done before. We put a diaphragm to go over the top of the missile to keep the water out, because we didn't want to wet the missile when you opened that hatch. It took a little thinking to come up with that and come up with one that you could break through and get the missile out after the water had gotten on the diaphragm. So that system had to be developed, and a lot of things came up with it. Each one of them had different things that had to be settled down and decide this was the way we wanted to go.

John T. Mason, Jr.: There must have been some sleepless nights in various households.

Mr. Buescher: There were some sleepless nights. The job I was trying to do at that time was make all of these guys work together where they interfaced with each other to help them solve their problem or solve it for them.

John T. Mason, Jr.: Yes, I'm glad that last time you did talk about the personnel aspects, because it's so terribly important. I keep thinking about the personnel as you talk about these programs.

Mr. Buescher: Now, I'm referring to the interfaces doing the development, I mean our contractors and our branches, where they have to go outside of their fence that I told you about to try to make them solve the problem. If they can't, then we do it for them at the system level.

John T. Mason, Jr.: Didn't you have some kind of a monkey wrench tossed into the time schedule with the Sputnik and so on?*

Mr. Buescher: It was. We had a time scale. We undertook this thing on a firm time scale, that we'd do it in such and such a time.

John T. Mason, Jr.: What was your original premise?

Mr. Buescher: You already asked me what was the diameter of the Jupiter missile we were trying to get in the submarine. That was 120 inches, and the Polaris that we finally put in there had a diameter of 54. The Jupiter was also 41.3 feet long, and our first Polaris was 28.5 feet long, much smaller. Our original development time scale was to deploy the first Polaris submarine and missiles in January of 1963. Things came along that kind of messed that up because the Russians had put up the first Sputnik and made the U.S. Defense Department realize that they had much more of a capability than was thought, not necessarily in missiles but a possibility of coming up with ballistic missiles. They asked us

---

* On 4 October 1957, the Soviet Union launched Sputnik I, the first artificial earth satellite. It caused great uproar in the United States, which had expected to be first in space.

what we could do, and I remember we started this development in 1956, and it was agreed that we would employ our first system. Instead of 1963, we were to deploy in late 1960.

John T. Mason, Jr.: That must have called for some intensive thinking and some conferences, did it not?

Mr. Buescher: We certainly went into fast time on it, I'll tell you, long hours and everything else. It took a complete reevaluation of the program to see what we could do and thought we would give this a try. Raborn and Admiral Burke, CNO at the time, agreed and presented this to the Secretary of Defense. That was bought, and more money was provided, and more authority was given. We met the date. Sometimes we were charging pretty hard, and sometimes people outside of the program couldn't understand what we were doing.

For instance, our first firings at the Cape Canaveral the missile blew up.[*] We had a rather high percentage of bad missiles out of the first ones we fired. More concerned elements in the Navy and elsewhere said, "Oh, stop the program. Let's find out." They didn't seem to understand the purpose of a test is to find out what is wrong. You don't go back on your drawing board until you've done everything you could up there. Something was happening and we had to find out about it. We just kept firing missiles and kept firing missiles, and gradually we improved and improved and improved and we got a real good one initially.

John T. Mason, Jr.: How did SP convince the conservative voice?

Mr. Buescher: I'm not sure we did convince them. It's just that we had enough backing, and there was enough priority on this program that the right people were convinced and had enough confidence in the people in the project to say, "Let's proceed." Every time you have a failure, you don't close everything down. What we were doing is we would get

---

[*] The first test firing of the Polaris AX-1 test vehicle, on 24 September 1958, was unsuccessful. The first successful firing was the AX-6; on 20 April 1959 it was flown 400 nautical miles down the Atlantic Missile Range. A shipboard test of the AX-22 followed on 27 August 1959 from the test ship <u>Observation Island</u> (EAG-154).

some inkling of what it might be that caused the problem, and we would just put more instrumentation on the missile and putting more coverage of the flight and much more intense evaluation of the flight data from flight to flight. We didn't always get this done between flights.

John T. Mason, Jr.: When did these tests begin?

Mr. Buescher: I think they must have started about 1958 or 1959. I don't have all of that data; I left it at SP. Anything on SP, you see, I left there. So the specifics of that I really can't tell you. But it must have been late 1958 or 1959. In the meantime, we were proceeding to put this missile in production.

John T. Mason, Jr.: That took a leap of faith, did it not?

Mr. Buescher: It took a lot of guts, I can tell you.

I might comment on something now. There is a fly-before-buy policy in the DoD, and that says develop it, then go out and have it evaluated, and then come back and once you've got the evaluation charted out, then go out and buy your tactical items. We've never worked that way. As I said, we were still having these terrible failures, and we were beginning to put the missile into production. Despite the excellent results we got with our Polaris, Poseidon, and Trident weapon systems, every time there's a new start on another weapon system generation, we have to fight the thing of, "Let's go out on a competitive bid; you've got to go through this fly-before-you-buy to protect tactical production." We had to fight it every time, and we had to actually get a waiver every time to fight it. We've never done it that way, and in our project it would add considerable cost, time, and risks to do so.

John T. Mason, Jr.: Was this because SP is the exception to the system?

Mr. Buescher: This was the way we know how to get the job done. We had so much success, such high reliability that it would be most difficult to do it another way and obtain similar results. What that does for you is this: you've got a whole group of people and activities working on the development, and in my opinion, that's the easiest part. You get any help you want from any source to solve those problems. And what do you end up with after the development program? You end up with a set of documents, a whole set of drawings and specifications and things of that sort which you would produce the equipment later on.

Now, you want all of the equipment going into production and going into the fleet to be the same, so you use one set of documentation. That's the reason I talked so much before about documentation. But if you bring it up to a point and get a set of documentation, and you think you've got it and you stop and make some test items and it takes two or three years—and that's what it takes—to evaluate them and get approval for production, you've lost your original team. You've just lost that team, and you've got a whole brand-new bunch of guys that don't know anything about the missiles taking that documentation to produce it. Sure, they make changes because they haven't developed their sense of producibility right yet, so they're going to make the changes that will make it easy for them to do their job. They don't have the design team left who will put a constraint on them and say, "Whoa, if you change that, it will make this much difference."

In most cases, when you end up with a set of documentation and you end up with a successful documentation program, that equipment works, but you don't fully know why it works. You don't know all of the aspects of why that thing works and what it is that makes it work. If you say, "I have a set of documentation which I have made these items of this documentation and I have controlled production processes and I have done all of these great things. . ." If you make it that way, you'll probably have a good item. You don't know every little change in a process for mixing propellants and things of this sort. So many little things could be changed and can affect the outcome and the performance of that thing. If you have the guys who had that knowledge, or the best there is, by the time you go through this fly-before-you-buy evaluation, you will have lost the knowledgeable design personnel.

John T. Mason, Jr.: You're really saying that Father Time is an element in this picture.

Mr. Buescher: That's right. Not only that, but you can't get the same materials, you can't get the same parts, and they go through substitutions and all of this. You've lost the interest of industry, and you have to go back not to the guys that you would have normally gone back to to produce this thing, but by the time you've gone through this and you have it on a competitive contract, you don't get the best guy necessarily on a competitive contract. You just get the lowest price, and that doesn't necessarily produce what you want.

John T. Mason, Jr.: You were talking about the tests and continue and also putting it into production simultaneously. Can you recall, in a sense, the aura of feeling among the important boys at that point? Was there any discouragement with the program, or were you still so optimistic that you were going to do it in spite of hell and high water?

Mr. Buescher: Well, we thought we'd do it. We knew we were. It was a question of what reliability we were going to get, whether it was going to he fully reliable or whether it wasn't going to meet those goals. We felt sure that we were on the right track in most all areas. We didn't want to be like the earlier Terrier and Tartar. I remember we talked about that the last time, where they had to redo it in order to produce it. They hadn't picked up this philosophy. That was before our time, but that's where a lot of us learned about this thing, as well as in small rocket programs.

    To my knowledge there was never in SP, or in the Navy, in the particular spots that controlled the programs, any feeling that we were not going to make it. We maybe might not meet all the goals, but we were going to come up with a ballistic missile, a deterrent missile and get it deployed, and we were going to try to get it deployed on that new date, on that accelerated date. Everybody was very enthused about it, and everybody was going just as hard as they could to get there, to meet that objective. I never saw anybody slow down because they had any feeling that they weren't going to make it. I never saw anybody discouraged or who thought they weren't going to make it, because everybody was very optimistic. You had a bunch of charging horses, and you couldn't slow them down, you see. We could have ended up with nothing, but that wasn't our feeling ever. It was a high-risk program, people hadn't done it before, but there was enough related experience in the program, and we had good, experienced people both in SP and outside in the contractors. We were determined that it was going to be.

John T. Mason, Jr.: What about the simultaneous development of the proper submarine, the real goal?

Mr. Buescher: Just as a sidelight, I remember when I left BuWeps to go to SP, this was one of the things that the higher-ups in BuWeps kept warning me about—getting into a program that was going to fail and that my whole reputation was going to be tarnished. That was partly because they believed it but partly to discourage me from leaving. It's kind of hard when people talk to you like that to go ahead and make the decision to leave, but I did.

John T. Mason, Jr.: Well, Levering Smith had left.

Mr. Buescher: Levering had left BuWeps many, many years ahead of that time. He had gone out to China Lake and then to White Sands. Many of the people who may have predicted failure and may have predicted chaos were people who didn't know how to run a program; they hadn't had any real experience. They had been hanging on the edges all of these years and had never really been involved to take any responsibility. So you kind of have to forget a lot of that stuff. There were a lot of doom-and-gloom people but not in the project, not in the project.

John T. Mason, Jr.: That I hoped you would have established as a point.

Mr. Buescher: Yes. Nor in the Navy as far as I know. If it was, it was in the part of the Navy that I had no dealings with.

John T. Mason, Jr.: Will you say something about the simultaneous preparation of an adequate vehicle, the submarine?

Mr. Buescher: The Polaris submarine was quite an undertaking, and it was quite a new concept, the way the Navy was going to do this, BuShips.[*] Rickover had developed and deployed a new fleet attack submarine with a particular nuclear power plant. The question was what to do about the submarine for the Polaris program. It looked as if the power plant was adequate to do the job, and I say, "Thank God that it was," because you had to have a new—and I mean really new—weapon system and not a simultaneous nuclear power plant development. It's very difficult to come up with two major developments at the same time in the same vehicle. I say, "Thank God BuShips had one" and could kind of step back and let SSPO take the lead on that thing.

The first time we really came up with that situation was in the Trident, where Rickover came up with a new power plant and SSPO developed a new weapon system in the same submarine.

John T. Mason, Jr.: Which still continue.

Mr. Buescher: Yes. They still continue. But it creates a problem in program management. It creates technical problems, and it creates a lot of things because if you take a power plant and you know its capacity and you know what kind of power it can furnish not only to the ship but to the weapon system, then you can go ahead and make agreements, and you come up with a development plan which makes those assumptions, you see. If you are working with a new development, an unknown power plant and every time you have a problem you have to go back and lay it on him as a problem for him to solve, too, simultaneously. You don't do that it you've already got one. And that's what it was. I would say off the shelf, but nothing is off the shelf, really.

It was an adaptation of an earlier submarine. They had one on the building ways at Electric Boat and once SP decided how many Polaris missiles and how big that missile compartment was going to be and BuShips ran through whatever they had to do to evaluate that power plant and the submarine with that additional length, then the plan was to take that SSBN on the ways at Groton, to cut it in half and insert this long missile compartment

---

[*] For the aspect of the program that involved design of the submarine, please see the Naval Institute oral history of Captain Harry A. Jackson, USN (Ret.).

in it and build in from there. That was a blessing. That was real fine. It wasn't easy. Even then it wasn't easy, but it cut down on a lot of problems, it cut down on a lot of management problems.

John T. Mason, Jr.: Did Rickover go along with this idea readily?

Mr. Buescher: Yes, once he decided that his power plant could do the job. He didn't really try to control anything from there.

John T. Mason, Jr.: You might for the record say how the decision was made on the number of missiles carried in this submarine and also, for the record, you might say who named the Polaris.

Mr. Buescher: Well, I believe Raborn named the program Polaris, at least that's always been my impression, that he came up with it simply because we needed the North Star as a reference, the Polaris.

John T. Mason, Jr.: This was a pseudo-astrologer?

Mr. Buescher: Yes, and it was pretty jazzy to call it Polaris, you see. Of course, you'd expect that from Raborn. It catches the imagination, you see. That answers one of your questions. The other question on how many missiles—every time there's a new submarine, that question comes up. As you know, the Trident submarine, the latest one, the big Trident submarine, has 24 missiles. The Polaris submarine had 16 in all, and the Poseidon had 16.

It comes down to the fact that you go through a whole bunch of studies and cost tradeoffs, operational tradeoffs, on what it takes to first acquire the system (that's to build the submarines and build the missiles and have the missile depots to support them and operational areas) how many areas are you going to operate in, how are you going to divide the submarine up in operational areas. All of these are factors in it, and there's no "yes or no" answer. It just comes down, after you get all of these facts, to somebody saying they think it ought to be 16 or 24. There's no hard-and-fast answer. It's a judgment call.

And that's what happened in the early days of Polaris. They went through all of these studies, and it was decided that to get the proper coverage the Navy needed and the U.S. needed, they would need 41 boats with 16 missiles each. You could say, "Well, why couldn't we have fewer boats and more missiles aboard each boat, keeping the same number of total missiles?" But when you look at it, you see that these boats are out for so long, they're in overhaul for so long and they're in a refit period between patrols for so long that it doesn't come out just that way. We also had a lot of different patrol areas; we had the Pacific and we had the Atlantic. If you made half as many and put them all in the Atlantic, that's not the same as having twice as many with fewer missiles and putting them in both oceans. That doesn't give you an answer, but it kind of tells you what went into it.

John T. Mason, Jr.: So you had the problem of overseas bases too.

Mr. Buescher: That had to do with the patrol area, where you were going to deploy them from. You had the Med, you had the North Atlantic, you had the Pacific and you had all these things.

John T. Mason, Jr.: It was a very complex picture.

Mr. Buescher: It was a complex picture and the Trident, when it came along, the picture changed considerably. It was decided that all these would be based in the U.S.; all Trident submarines would be based in the U.S.

John T. Mason, Jr.: So you no longer need the bases for Trident.

Mr. Buescher: Well, not only don't you need them; you don't want them there. You get longer-range missiles, you get longer-range submarines. We also have the longer-range ASW coverage and we want to keep SSBNs back out of range. As time goes on, you want to keep those submarines back so they can operate out of the U.S. even better than operating out of a foreign base. The foreign bases are more vulnerable.

John T. Mason, Jr.: There's more security at home too.

Mr. Buescher: What the Russians do and how they become armed and their capabilities, as they get better, the whole concept of these things can change—not just what we'd like to do but also what we think they're doing or know they're doing.

John T. Mason, Jr.: Now, you got the Polaris developed and the first submarine was launched. The George Washington was launched in 1959.*

Mr. Buescher: I'm going to repeat something I told you the other day. We were very worried about getting that submarine to sea and getting that weapon system to sea. I think we touched a bit on the Navy's experience up to that time. They could get the ship to look and act like a ship, but they couldn't get their weapons to work. We were very worried about that, and we decided to do it differently than the way it had been done. We felt we could do it better, and we felt that not knowingly, but in hindsight, they had made some errors of judgment in how they had managed the program. We felt it was SP's job to make sure it got done and done right, that when that submarine came out of the shipyard, it had to be ready to fire missiles. Not like many other programs, where they had had to take these ships, after the ship was operational, to put it in another shipyard for two or three years to make the weapon system work.

John T. Mason, Jr.: This is readiness underscored, isn't it?

Mr. Buescher: Readiness underscored. The problem was that in earlier programs all of these weapon subsystems, all of these equipments were shipped to the shipbuilder, and he was given the job of getting them installed, checked out, and operating the way they should. That required a tremendous and impossible job of transfer of knowledge to that

---

* The keel for the ballistic missile submarine George Washington (SSBN-598) was laid on 1 November 1957. She was launched on 9 June 1959 and commissioned on 30 December 1959. Her first deterrent patrol began in November 1960. She served until being decommissioned on 24 January 1985.

shipbuilder. That is not his specialty; his specialty is ships, so why give him the job of making the weapon system work?

John T. Mason, Jr.: There is something lost in the transition.

Mr. Buescher: There's a lot lost, a lot lost. The thing that was controlling that shipyard as it is today is, "When do I get that ship to sea?"—the date of when to get that ship to sea, not the date when it goes to sea and everything works right including the weapon system—just when will that ship go to sea. That's what the shipbuilder's paid to do, to get that ship to sea.

So we set up a program (and I had a very heavy hand in this one) where we retained control. We would ship all of this equipment to the shipyard, and we would put our people there with certain defined responsibilities and not hazy about who was to do what. We spelled out exactly what our responsibilities were to get this to work.

John T. Mason, Jr.: Was there any opposition there in developing this idea?

Mr. Buescher: There may have been, but we as a total team were running so hard on it that it was not a major issue. We set our teams up in the shipyard; we checked out our equipments as a subsystem before we ever shipped them and knew they were working as a subsystem. Where necessary, we set up a mating test to some degree in our subsystem contractor's plants—not big tests, but where we could without shipping everything. We'd just ship certain things. For instance, all of this instrumentation that we were going to use in the shipyard, to install and put in the shipyard and use to take data on, these are temporary installations, to take data from the tests we were going to run on all of this equipment in the shipyard. We shipped that, for instance, to GE so we could mate it up with fire control and get the bugs out of that as much as we could. The same kind of stuff that checked out the missiles we had that missile contractor check it out. It was all to get that equipment operating and working in the ship's environment where there's a different wiring and different hookups and different conditions and different people. It's quite different.

So we set up our shipyard test teams. Each subsystem team and my system personnel at Vitro helping me, we set up a team in the shipyard and these teams would really honcho this whole job through. We didn't just let the equipment be shipped to the shipbuilder and then go into his storage and that's it. We had our guys down there verifying that it got there. We would ship it on our trucks to the shipyard, and we would not ship it until he was ready to install it.

The shipbuilder likes to have everything there two or three years ahead of time so that nobody slows him up. When he's ready to do something, it's there in his storage. We wouldn't agree to that. We said, "No, that's not the way to do it. You give us 30 days' notice, and we'll have that equipment right there, ready to go down in the submarine."

John T. Mason, Jr.: Hand-carried.

Mr. Buescher: Sentry hand-carried, you see. Not only that, we've got the team there working in the shipyard who understands what's happening there. They've been kind of watching the shipbuilder to make sure he's putting the wiring in right, that he's following the plan that we've worked out, and we've come up with a set of coordination drawings to say this is the way it ought to be. It may be nothing more than a hole in the deck that big in order to get air-conditioning in. But it's in the right place, and it's big enough and so and so forth. It may be a certain kind of cabling or a ship-installed communication from one compartment to the other. We're watching all of these things, you see.

And we set up a test program to do it piece by piece, phase by phase. We'd say, "Shipbuilder, this is not acceptable. You do it." On the old way, the inspector at the shipyard said okay. But we said we were going to test each of these services and each of these things. It may be a wire or an electrical output or anything. It may be air-conditioning for the room and temperature. Whatever he does, we check on this thing, and we've got a team here working with him under his control. Normally, SP controlled it.

John T. Mason, Jr.: You weren't fooling him.

Mr. Buescher: We weren't fooling him. It went better in a rather businesslike way and a very practical way to make sure that everybody did the job right. We had a way of checking to see that they did it. We set up the right tests, we came up with a tolerance for the test. Nobody could waive a test that didn't come back to us (SP). Nobody could do away with a test without coming back to us. They couldn't run their tests without having all the right people there to watch it, to record it. We're talking about all of our subsystems contractors, my systems contractor and supervised by the supervisor of shipbuilding, who was a Navy guy on the spot. We're all there, part of a team to run this thing and get it done right. We just went through the whole shipbuilding program that way.

Out of all the ships that have gone through the shipyard being built and overhauled a new system installed—not just 41. Every one of them has been through several overhauls, and some had been converted to Poseidon. Every single one of them has left that shipyard and has been able to go down and fire a missile the way it ought to. That's quite an accomplishment, quite an accomplishment. Again, it gets back to that looking at detail. I talk about details in terms of correspondence and signature authority. That was typical of the same type of detail we were watching and trying to control throughout the whole thing. We wouldn't just say, "Well, that's your job," to the shipbuilder. It was our job as a program manager to get the thing done, and we will maintain the overall control of it. We weren't taking away from the shipbuilder anything. We were giving him all kinds of help. It's true that it was held to also watch him. He was helped to get the test run the way we wanted it and make sure the things were operating.

John T. Mason, Jr.: But somewhere along the line the shipbuilder himself must have entered into the spirit of the thing.

Mr. Buescher: He did, he did. He entered into the spirit of the thing, not without reservations, of course, because this is a new way of him doing things.

John T. Mason, Jr.: Because this was really a national spirit.

Mr. Buescher: I remember one time I had a hell of a run-in with a Navy skipper who was the commanding officer of the first ship. The old way when the ship was built, somewhere along the way during the latter stage of contraction the supervisor of shipbuilding turned over control to the commanding officer of the ship. He didn't have the right kind of people to manage that thing and supervise the shipbuilding, who had been double-hatted on Raborn's staff. They turned it over to the commanding officer of the ship, and he started saying what tests were going to be run and what were not going to be run and all this. I had quite a run-in with that guy. For a while, he wasn't speaking to me. But that didn't make any difference; it got the job done. We ended up friends before it was over with.

That whole shipbuilding program, as you might imagine, as time went on tensions began to build up. We had six phases of this test program. As time went on, the tension built up and built up. I remember one day we were running a countdown. A countdown is when you start at T-minus-15 minutes, and you run right through the launch sequence to make sure things were operating right. We ran that several times, and every time we had to stop; it wasn't working.

It got to the point where people were almost fighting, just over the edge, you know. All these guys were running around there, sharp with each other and quarrelling with each other aboard that ship. So we said, "Stop, everybody go home, get the hell out of this shipyard, go home, get drunk, get a good night's sleep and then come back tomorrow and we'll run it again." That's what happened. The next day, on the first try, we successfully completed the countdown. But, you know, it had reached a point where there was too much happening. But that's part of it, and you kind of expect it to happen.

John T. Mason, Jr.: It's the application of human psychology.

Mr. Buescher: Yes. We could have run it 20 more times that day, and everybody was on such an edge that we wouldn't have gotten it. Somebody would have kept doing something wrong. It wasn't necessarily the equipment that was wrong; it was the people doing things.

John T. Mason, Jr.: The Polaris submarine is launched and is under way and the others are being turned out according to schedule, the numbers.

Mr. Buescher: That's right.

John T. Mason, Jr.: Where along the line did SP decide that A-1 had to become A-2?

Mr. Buescher: Let me think about that one. I know exactly when it happened. When we took the acceleration of the program, when we cut out two years originally—originally we were supposed to have a system ready for evaluation in 1965, and it turned out that the change was that we would have a tactical deployed system in 1961. So that was a big hunk of time they took out. But the missile we came up with had a range of 1,200 nautical miles. It was felt by the Navy and DoD that we should try to get a 1,500-nautical-mile missile. So about the time that the acceleration was accepted, it was also a requirement for a longer-range missile to be established for 1,500 nautical miles.

John T. Mason, Jr.: That was the determining factor of the range?

Mr. Buescher: Yes. That was the A-2 missile. We put a new fuel stage motor on it on the A-1. But everything up front was essentially the same. An A-2 required a change of a launcher system to make it handle a longer missile. It required some fire control changes, and it required a change in the missile, of course. When I said launcher, I meant the ship too. We also came up with a new class submarine when we went to the A-2, the 608 class, I believe it was, when we put the A-2 in.*

At the same time, when they came up with a 1,500-mile missile there was a longer-range requirement established for 2,400-nautical miles missile, which later became the A-3. We didn't just do the A-1 and then stop and wonder what was going to happen.

John T. Mason, Jr.: You had no stationary period, did you?

Mr. Buescher: No. The A-2 was a minimum change program. It still cost a lot of money and a lot of effort, you see, but the fact that we were making the missile longer required some development of the missile and some of these other things. But it didn't require new concepts. A-3 did. A-3 came along as a multiple warhead. I've forgotten all of these

---

* USS Ethan Allen (SSBN-608) was commissioned 8 August 1961 as the first of her class.

dates. Things were happening so fast and so furiously, you know, I'd have to stop and think about it a little bit.

John T. Mason, Jr.: What was the compelling factor that forced SP to constantly project for the future?

Mr. Buescher: It wasn't just SP, it was the Navy and the DoD, the whole Defense Department. As new intelligence would come in as to what the enemy's—the Russians'—defensive capability changes that occurred or they could contemplate how a system could be defeated, then this whole thing was wrung out over a period of time with SP participating but not leading. We were in there pretty deep, but it was not our study. The studies were a CNO requirement and the DoD requirement as to what should be coming along in order to protect this capability.

John T. Mason, Jr.: I suppose you can very adequately use the word race. It was a race.

Mr. Buescher: It was a race. We were trying to project ahead as to what we'd need to keep ahead of this game. That has characterized every single one of them: A-1, A-2, A-3, C-3, C-4 and D-5. Every single one of them is the same way.

John T. Mason, Jr.: The C's being the Poseidons?

Mr. Buescher: Well, C is Poseidon, yes.

John T. Mason, Jr.: A-3 was not, was it?

Mr. Buescher: A-3 is what we called the Polaris.

John T. Mason, Jr.: Would you at this point tell me, for the record again, the distinction between multiple warhead and MIRV, as it's used nowadays.[*]

---

[*] MIRV—multiple, independently targeted reentry vehicle.

Mr. Buescher: That's a funny thing. I started reading about this terrible MIRV stuff in the papers and all this controversy. I hadn't really realized that we were the bad boys. We were the ones putting out the MIRV missile, you see. I didn't understand it under those names, you see.

John T. Mason, Jr.: Well, there is a distinction, isn't there?

Mr. Buescher: You can have a multiple warhead, but you also have multiple warheads in each of those warheads of maneuverable afterwards, you see. Multiple warheads you just aim and they separate and they go, but you can cause a MIRV missile to drop some warheads here and then continue flying and then drop some more and you can drop them in patterns. That's what the MIRV is.

John T. Mason, Jr.: When you pushed ahead to the A-3, you had the multiple warheads.

Mr. Buescher: That's right, but it was the Poseidon, the C-3, where we came up with the MIRV.

John T. Mason, Jr.: Did you have a hand in the development of the multiple warheads?

Mr. Buescher: Not the warhead itself, no.

John T. Mason, Jr.: Did you have a hand in the discussion of the idea before it actually developed?

Mr. Buescher: Well, yes, sort of on the edges, mostly from the standpoint of the total system, not specifically from the warhead itself, but what would that do to the system, could we accommodate a missile outfitted that way in the system, what kind of changes did we have to make to the system? The system is everything but the missile. From that standpoint, yes. And it did require changes, and it did impose requirements on the rest of the weapon system.

John T. Mason, Jr.: The A-3 had a range of what?

Mr. Buescher: The A-3 had 2,500 nautical miles.

John T. Mason, Jr.: And then they weren't satisfied with that.

Mr. Buescher: The C-3, I believe, was about the same range. The C-4 went somewhere beyond that.

John T. Mason, Jr.: And as you say, the C's are the Poseidon.

Mr. Buescher: The Poseidon.

John T. Mason, Jr.: This didn't entail an entirely new submarine, however.

Mr. Buescher: No, we kept the same submarines all the way up through C-4.

John T. Mason, Jr.: Weren't there some conversions of A-3?

Mr. Buescher: The 598 class, which had the A-1, were never backfitted for any other kind of missile.

John T. Mason, Jr.: Would you explain that term "backfit"?

Mr. Buescher: Backfit means modifying an existing Polaris SSBN to take a different type missile. It requires different ship's services; it may require more room inside to accommodate a larger diameter missile and a greater length missile, and there is a difference in the launching characteristics for the launch system. The 608 class originally went out with the A-2 missiles and was converted for C-3 missiles later on, after they had been deployed for a few years and came back and got the C-3. First they got the A-3, then the C-3. The 626 was built originally for the A-3.* We always had in mind we'd have 41, and as time came along, the thing that was available at the time that the 616 class was going to be built, the missile that we put in it first was the A-3. Some of these were backfitted for C-3 and some of them were backfitted for C-4.

The missile that's going to be deployed in the big Trident submarine is a missile that is already being deployed in some of these converted ships, of the original 41. The D-5, which is the second-generation Trident, will be a larger missile, usable only in the larger Trident submarines. It's a. much bigger diameter.

John T. Mason, Jr.: So actually that's a whole new instrument of war—the submarine and the weapon.

Mr. Buescher: Yes the first Trident missile (C-4) was built with a length and diameter as to permit the backfitting of it into the early Polaris submarines. When we put the C-4 in the Trident submarine, the bigger Trident submarine, the possible launch tube diameter designed in the submarine for the missile was much larger. The C-4 missile didn't take all that room up. So when the longer D-5 missile is developed, we will backfit a larger launch tube for the D-5 missile.

John T. Mason, Jr.: Yes, what is the life of a submarine?

Mr. Buescher: As a general rule 20 years, but the Navy is working to improve that, and a longer life seems to be reasonable.

John T. Mason, Jr.: That's gratifying to know because of the amount of money invested.

Mr. Buescher: Your question was what was the life of a submarine.

John T. Mason, Jr.: Yes.

---

* The first eight submarines of the Ethan Allen (SSBN-616) class initially deployed with the Polaris A-2 missile. Later ships in the class, starting with the Daniel Webster (SSBN-626), carried the Polaris A-3. All were converted in the 1970s to carry Poseidon missiles.

Mr. Buescher: That's right. The life of a submarine depends primarily on ship-installed things such as piping, sea valves, things of this sort that affect the safety of the submarine and equipments affected by seawater. If you say what is the life of the weapons system, we don't hesitate to say that 20 or 30 years is reasonable.

John T. Mason, Jr.: A-3 missiles were first deployed in 1964.

Mr. Buescher: The A-3 missile was first deployed in September of 1964 on the SSBN-626. The A-3 missiles are still deployed by the U.K. today. But the things that affect missile life are those things that tend to change on their own, such as the chemicals within the propellant, or things that would cause cracking of the propellants and things of this sort. And rubber items tend to go bad.

John T. Mason, Jr.: And fatigue of metals and things.

Mr. Buescher: Not so much fatigue of metals, more of the organic type materials that you use. So it's almost 20 years, but there's a limited life on them. The rest of the weapon system will probably go 20 or 30 years, just taking a number out of the air. In the submarine, the things that are limited are valves and pipes and things that are affected by seawater that tend to rust or corrode or come apart.

John T. Mason, Jr.: Would you say then that one of the paramount factors in replacing a system is actually the pushing forward spirit, the competition?

Mr. Buescher: It is. It's a need for a change in military requirements requiring new systems with new capabilities is the thing that limits it. We haven't gone away from them because they're old; it's because they don't have the capabilities that later on the military characteristics have determined to be necessary in them, you see. As the enemy capability changes, your capabilities have to change, and you've got to match those things. It's a leapfrog thing.

John T. Mason, Jr.: Your range requirements are enlarged.

Mr. Buescher: Your range requirements and all of these things. The defense requirements are what dictate this whole thing, not the fact that we think it's going to go bad. You know that eventually they will. Nothing keeps on forever, and we know that particularly missiles are not, and submarines are not, but we go on and on.

John T. Mason, Jr.: Living with this series of developments in missiles, would you say in your own opinion that there is a limit beyond which you cannot go?

Mr. Buescher: A limit in what way?

John T. Mason, Jr.: In terms of size, for example.

Mr. Buescher: No, there's no limit. There is on how far you need to go. The earlier strategic ballistic missile went much longer.

John T. Mason, Jr.: I hear criticism on the size of the present missile under development and so forth.[*] Even Arleigh himself has talked about that.[†] He's very pessimistic about the size.

Mr. Buescher: We're talking about the submarine?

John T. Mason, Jr.: Yes.

Mr. Buescher: We've had so much trouble with that in the submarine, trying to get it built. It's going to be a tremendous thing at sea—the detectability of it, whether or not it's

---
[*] USS Ohio (SSBN-726), the first of a class of nuclear powered submarines armed with the Trident ballistic missile, was approved in the early 1970s. She was laid down 10 April 1976, launched 7 April 1979, and commissioned 11 November 1981. The ship is 560 feet long and displaces 18,750 tons submerged.
[†] This is a reference to Admiral Arleigh A. Burke, USN (Ret.), CNO from 1955 to 1961.

detectable by underwater means by Soviet submarines. An awful lot has been done to quiet it down.

John T. Mason, Jr.: But doesn't this fit in with my question, isn't there a time when you can reach a limit, an outer space, so to speak?

Mr. Buescher: I don't know what it is, though. If that submarine has been built on time, nobody would have been complaining. But now that it wasn't and now that it's been so late, everybody criticizes the hell out of it, you see. It isn't such a big thing, but they introduced a lot of new things in it, I'll tell you that.

John T. Mason, Jr.: That was getting involved with the shipbuilding contracts, wasn't it, the delay?

Mr. Buescher: They're pushing technology too, you know, in this new submarine in an awful lot of ways. They set up a bad contract, and I don't want to get involved with that. Too much has been said about it already and too many fights have gone on. That's not my area.

John T. Mason, Jr.: But wasn't that a factor in the delay and all the rest?

Mr. Buescher: In my opinion, they set up the wrong kind of contract.

John T. Mason, Jr.: Financing, that kind of thing.

Mr. Buescher: The first contract for the building of the submarine was a fixed-price contract. You don't do it that way. That's the wrong way, in my opinion. You're still developing that submarine.

John T. Mason, Jr.: So you can't envision the totality.

Mr. Buescher: Things are going to change, you see, before it gets its final specification and it's the old fly-before-buy. You can't do it. They should have made it CPFF for a while. I mean, the first one should have been a cost-plus-fixed-fee so they could introduce all these things and make all of these modifications and wouldn't have to fight about every single nitpicking change. If they had done that with a cost-plus-fixed-fee and then follow-on contracts of a different type—I don't say it has to be a fixed price; it could be a lot of contracts to push the contractor to give you more for your money.

What they had at EB, and still have, is have a part of the company who does the design of the submarine, and then they have another part of the company who they furnish the design to and they're the production outfit.* They have two different contracts, and these guys over here keep making the necessary changes, giving them to the Navy and the Navy gives them to the other side of EB, you see. Every time a change comes through, they want to renegotiate the fixed-price contract. I don't blame them. That's natural. That's what a fixed-price contract is, a contract that says he'll deliver it on time within a certain amount of money and in accordance of that design, not all of these changes.

John T. Mason, Jr.: Meanwhile the wages go up and all the rest of it.

Mr. Buescher: Not only that, but there's inflation; the changes in design have to be made. If some way that tactical submarine were built other than on a fixed-price contract, I think they would have been better off. That's not my area.

John T. Mason, Jr.: Tell me, we were just discussing off tape, I was asking you for some sort of a prognosis on ballistic missiles, the fact that we have such effective ones in being and how they might well guarantee, in a sense, the maintenance of peace in the world.

Mr. Buescher: I don't know if it can do anything to guarantee it.

John T. Mason, Jr.: I know that's a pretty good strong word.

---

* EB—the Electric Boat Division of the General Dynamics Corporation is a long-time submarine building yard in Groton, Connecticut.

Mr. Buescher: If there's going to be a nuclear war, it's going to be people who do it, and you can't always judge what people are going to decide to do, no matter what the consequences. I remember at the time of the Cuban crisis, the project received a letter from Kennedy which gave us an awful lot of credit as a very needed deterrent that helped settle that down to come to a peaceful solution on that.[*] I think all of us who worked in the project, me for 25 years, feel that we've made one large contribution, a very large contribution, to the deterrence of a nuclear war. We're not only talking about now but in the future as well.

John T. Mason, Jr.: You don't conceive of the development of this weapon as an aggressive act?

Mr. Buescher: We never did, we never did. We always speak of it as a deterrent, and that's what I feel it is today—a deterrent. The fact that it is a seagoing weapon that could be essentially hidden in the ocean makes it very hard to detect, very hard to defeat. It just has to be for many years to come a great, and one of the major, reasons why it would be foolish to get into a nuclear war for the enemy.

John T. Mason, Jr.: Do you see a time in the future when detection will be developed to the point where it isn't any longer possible to hide it, so to speak?

Mr. Buescher: It will make it harder to hide. As times goes on, if the Russians put a lot of time and money and effort in ASW detection, detection of things at long ranges, we still can move back by a coastline, and that's a much larger area that they have to search. Depending on how much they do and how much they put into it, it certainly increases detectability of the systems. But we're not going to stand still either, you know. D-5 is probably not the last generation, either.

---

[*] The Cuban Missile Crisis was triggered in mid-October 1962, when a U.S. reconnaissance plane photographed a Soviet nuclear missile site in Cuba and the presence of Soviet bombers. On 22 October President John F. Kennedy went on national television to announce a naval quarantine of Cuba, to be implemented on 24 October. On 28 October Premier Nikita Khrushchev of the Soviet Union notified President Kennedy that he was ordering the withdrawal of Soviet bombers and missiles from Cuba.

John T. Mason, Jr.: No, one can speculate that perhaps there's something else on the drawing board.

Mr. Buescher: It depends on what's coming along and what is felt to be the need, and then you turn to the leapfrog thing, we jump ahead of them again, you see.

John T. Mason, Jr.: You personally must feel very good about devoting 25 years of your life to this project.

Mr. Buescher: I think when I made my little retirement speech, that's one thing I said. I was very satisfied with my career with the Navy, and I was particularly satisfied working with SP, a very dedicated group who made a very, very large contribution to the security of this country. I really mean it, and I still feel that way. You can go on working forever, but after 40 years, I felt it was time for me to move along and do something else. I had 25 years in SP. That was the reason I retired, not that it still wasn't a challenge and a very interesting assignment. But you can't stay forever. Some day you have to train people who come behind you, and you have to pick a good time to leave. So I tried to take all of that into consideration when I decided to retire, rather than just up and quit. I've retired three times now.

John T. Mason, Jr.: You've just recently retired again.

Mr. Buescher: That was a short one, but I had to go through the retirement again.

John T. Mason, Jr.: Did you make another speech?

Mr. Buescher: No, they didn't give me another party either.

John T. Mason, Jr.: Well, I do thank you very much.

Mr. Buescher: It's been a real pleasure, and I've enjoyed doing this. I had no idea what it was all about when we started, but I hope I've been helpful.

John T. Mason, Jr.: You have indeed.

Index to the Oral History of
Mr. John B. Buescher

Air Force, U.S.
MX Peacekeeper development (1980s), 37–38; Jupiter missile operational use and control (1959), 110–112

Ammunition
Bureau of Ordnance procurement and production projects (early 1940s), 6–8; VT fuze development during World War II by John Hopkins Applied Physics Lab, 6, 9, 35, 51; program management (1940s-1950s), 7–8; design control importance to quality and uniformity, 13, 50–52; procurement and production projects (early 1940s), 14; test strategies, 17–18; quality control of, 20; explosive ordnance disposal work (early 1940s), 29–30; standardization program with the United Kingdom (3.75-inch gun) (late 1940s), 27–29; offshore ammunition procurement programs from foreign countries (early 1950s), 23–25; procurement and production projects in early 1940s, 35–36; shelf-life of ammunition meant ample supplies were on hand at beginning of Korean War, 41

Anti-tank rocket
Development spurred by BuOrd by start of Korean War in 1950, 38–40

Applied Physics Laboratory/Johns Hopkins University (APL/JHU)
Role in naval ordnance development (1940s and 1950s), 6, 9, 33

Buescher, John B.
Family background, 1; education, 2; children, 42–45; Washington area residence, 21–22; beginning of employment at the Bureau of Ordnance (BuOrd) in 1941, 3; on lack of flexibility in government programs, 5; production-engineer duties at BuOrd, 7–8; bosses and mentors at BuOrd, 9, 10, 13; career path timeline, 10–11; on the complex nature of systems development and operational deployment, 11-12; on the importance of design control and coordination at BuOrd, 13, 50–52; sense of duty to deployed personnel, 14; scope of duties at the BuOrd, 16–17; quality control duties, 18–20; on ease of working with civilian contractors, 21; on converting designs from metric to standard measurement, 35-37; project management after reorganization (mid 1950s), 46–49; funding procurement strategy at BuOrd, 49; personal contacts at SP, 52, 53; on the non-specific nature of his job description, 53–55; beginning of employment at SP (late 1955), 53; bosses and mentors at SP, 54, 105–106; position at SP, 69; on the pressing need for overall program control and coordination, 55–57; on Rear Admiral William Raborn's personality and management techniques, 58–61; Saturday meetings with Raborn, 59–60; on working relationship with Gordon Pehrson, 61–62; on working relationship with contractors, 64, 67–72; coordination drawings concept initiated at SP, 66–67, 72–73; on rationale for specific contractor selections, 71; on working relationship with bureaus, 72; on the need for complete design control and full-design disclosure, 73–75; staff selection, 74; opposition to a reliance on

competitive bidding, 84–86, 124, 126; on the long-term success of SP's quality control approach, 92; personal satisfaction and pride derived from long-term work at SP, 96; on need to take care of personnel, 101–102; on the benefits of consistency from low-personnel turnover, 104–105; start of work on a solid-propellant missile (1956), 112; on the dedication and positive attitude of SP programs participants, 126–127; decision to leave BuOrd (late 1955), 127; on the necessity of keeping up with changes in military requirements, 141–142; life of a weapons system description, 141; on the problems with a current submarine program, 142–144; on the value of deterrent-based weapons systems, 145; on decision to retire, 146. *See also* Bureau of Ordnance (BuOrd); Special Projects Office (SP)

BuOrd
See Bureau of Ordnance (BuOrd)

Bureau of Naval Weapons (BuWeps)
Formed in 1959 by merger of Bureau of Aeronautics and Bureau of Ordnance, 3, 46

Bureau of Ordnance (BuOrd)
Buescher on post-World War II change from design to managerial duties at BuOrd, 3–4; projects in early 1940s, 6–8, 14, 35–36; VT fuze effort (mid-1940s), 6, 9, 35, 51; program management (1940s-1950s), 7–8; civilian contractors for, 7–9; design control importance to quality and uniformity, 13, 50–52; impact of lack of configuration control on torpedo quality (World War II), 15–16, 50–51; testing of ammunition, 17–18; quality control duties, 18–20; offshore ammunition procurement programs (early 1950s), 23–25; rocket programs (late 1940s), 26–27; Sidewinder development work (early 1950s), 26–27, 31; post-World War II period work, 26; technical management group work (late 1940s), 26; ammunition standardization program with the United Kingdom (3.75-inch gun) (late 1940s), 27–29; explosive ordnance disposal work (1940s), 29–30; missile systems production work (early 1950s), 32–33; anti-tank shaped-charge rocket development (Korean War), 38–40; shelf-life of ammunition meant ample supplies were on hand at beginning of Korean War, 41; funding procurement strategy used by Buescher, 49; torpedo program problems, 50–51

Canberra (CAG-2)
Guided missile heavy cruiser that had problems with her missile systems when commanded by Captain Reich (1960-1961), 81

China Lake (Naval Ordnance Test Station)
Development work for BuOrd (1940s and 1950s), 27, 31, 35, 39

Civilian defense contractors
BuOrd projects in early 1940s, 7–9; design control by BuOrd and, 13; quality control by BuOrd and, 19–20; ease of working with, 21; offshore ammunition procurement programs (foreign countries) (early 1950s), 23–25; for anti-tank missile components during Korean War, 40; Polaris missile program role (late 1950s), 5; working relationship with SP, 67–72; Buescher's opposition to a reliance on competitive

bidding, 84–86, 124, 126; evaluation system used by SP to maintain contractor quality, 89–91

Cuban Missile Crisis
President John Kennedy sent the Special Projects Office a letter at the time of the 1962 crisis to credit the deterrent value of Polaris, 145

Daniel Webster USS (SSBN-626)
Polaris ballistic missile first deployed on this submarine (1964), 140

Department of Defense (DoD)
Disagreement with SP over tight quality standards being used by SP (late 1950s - early 1960s), 91–92

Electric Boat Division, General Dynamics Corporation
Coordination with SP on Polaris weapon system, 83–84, 144

Explosive ordnance disposal
BuOrd's role in 1940s in developing gadgets used in disposal projects, 29–30

George Washington USS (SSBN-598)
Concern in the late 1950s in the Special Projects Office that the ship and Polaris weapon system would work together, 131

Great Britain
Ammunition (3.75-inch gun) standardization program with BuOrd (late 1940s), 27–29; Buescher's trip to London during ammunition production program with NATO nations (early 1950s), 24–25; initiation into SP coordination and control policies for joint Polaris program (early 1960s), 106–109

Guns
BuOrd oversight of 20mm and 40mm gun manufacture in US (early 1940s), 35; joint U.S.-Great Britain 3.75-inch gun development to fit standardized rounds of ammunition (late 1940s, early 1950s), 27–29

See also Ammunition, Bureau of Ordnance

Hussey, Rear Admiral George F., Jr., USN (USNA, 1916)
Duties as Chief of the Bureau of Ordnance during World War II, 9, 22–23

Jupiter Missile
Liquid-propellant missile considered and rejected as viable for submarine-launched missile use (1955), 52, 110–112; dimensions, 122

Juran, Joseph M.
As one of the nation's top experts in quality control, made useful contributions in the

late 1950s to the Polaris development program, 76

Korean War
BuOrd spurred to high-priority development of anti-tank rockets due to use of tanks by Korea when the war began in 1950, 38–40; ample supply of ammunition on hand for, 41

Lubelsky, Captain Benjamin L., USN
Established quality control division in the Bureau of Ordnance during World War II, 18, 50

MIRV
See Multiple, Independently Targeted Reentry Vehicle

Missiles
Navy's decision to develop a solid-propellant missile (1956), 52–53; Sidewinder development (1950s), 26–27, 31; Talos, Tartar, and Terrier development (1950s), 32–33, 80–81; submarine-launched ballistic missiles development programs (1950s +), 36–37; Trident development (1970s), 36–37; MX Peacekeeper development (1980s), 37–38

See also Rockets; Submarine-launched ballistic missiles

Multiple, independently targeted reentry vehicle (MIRV)
Introduced to the Navy inventory with the Poseidon ballistic missile in the 1970s, 137–138

Naval Gun Factory, Washington, D.C.
Worked closely with the Bureau of Ordnance during World War II, 7, 20–21

Naval Ordnance Test Station (China Lake) (NOTS)
Development work for BuOrd (1940s and 1950s), 27, 31, 35, 39

Naval Proving Ground, Dahlgren, Virginia
Post-World War II role in testing guns and ammunition, 6, 17, 34–35, 39

North Atlantic Treaty Organization (NATO)
BuOrd contract with NATO nations for ammunition production (early 1950s), 23–25

Operational Test and Evaluation Force (OpTEvFor)
Tested several BuOrd projects but no Polaris involvement (1950s), 34, 35

Ordnance, Bureau of
See Bureau of Ordnance (BuOrd)

Peacekeeper, MX
Intercontinental ballistic missile (achieved operational capability in 1986), 37–38

Pehrson, Gordon O.
Good manager on the Polaris program but had clashes with branch heads in late 1950s, 61–62

Personnel
Submarine crew rotation concept, 79

Polaris ballistic missile
First submarine-launched ballistic missile (operational in 1960s), 4; shelf-life, 41; program name origin, 129; dimensions, 76, 111; consideration and rejection of liquid-propellant Jupiter missile (1955), 110–112; selection trade-off studies (early 1956), 112–113; introduction of redundancy to critical systems with full wartime capability as the goal (1956), 113–114; management focus on subsystem level of control, 114–117; program management and technical challenges of developing project, 119–121; early test results and repercussions (1958-1959), 123–124; U.S.-U.K. joint program management (early 1960s), 106–109; development time scale changed from deployment in 1963 to deployment in 1960 due to Sputnik, 122–123; documentation and controlled production processes used to ensure consistency and continuity, 125–126; success due to the dedication and positive attitude of participants, 126–127; evolution of power interface and numbers deployed decision, 128–130; direct and on-site involvement of SP with shipyards and weapon system installation and testing, 132–135; change to A-2 and A-3 programs, 136–137; system designations and conversions, 137, 139–140; first deployed on the submarine Daniel Webster (1964), 141; system life, 141

Poseidon missile
Submarine-launched ballistic missile (operational in 1970), 4, 137, 139–140

Raborn, Rear Admiral William F., Jr., USN (USNA, 1928)
SP directorship (1955-1962), 52; personality and management techniques, 58–61; management role when Jupiter missile was being considered (1955), 110; naming of Polaris program, 129; reputation as a good PR man and impact of his retirement on SP, 105–106

Reich, Rear Admiral Eli T., USN (USNA, 1935)
Leadership of effort to improve reliability of 3-T missiles (early 1960s), 33, 50, 81; commander of guided missile heavy cruiser Canberra (CAG-2) (1960-1961), 81

Richelieu (French battleship)
U.S. produced ammunition for this ship after she joined the Allied cause in World War II, 35–36

Rickover, Admiral Hyman G., USN (USNA, 1922)
Father of nuclear Navy, 80; training program for nuclear officers, 98

Rockets
BuOrd projects (early 1940s), 6–7; BuOrd programs (late 1940s), 26–27; BuOrd missile systems production work (early 1950s), 32–33; antisubmarine, 32; anti-tank shaped-charge rocket development (Korean War), 38–40

See also Missiles

Schoeffel, Rear Admiral Malcolm F., USN (USNA, 1919)
Bureau of Ordnance duties (1940s and 1950s), 10, 23–24

Sheppa, Milton
Civil service engineer in the Bureau of Ordnance during World War II, 13–14

Sidewinder
Air-to-air missile developed by the Bureau of Ordnance (1950s), 26–27, 31

Skybolt Missile
Program cancelled in 1962 leaving the British high and dry, 108–109

Smith, Rear Admiral Levering, USN (USNA, 1932)
Polaris missile project management based on subsystem level of control (late 1950s), 115–116; Work on rocket propellants at BuOrd (1940s), 10; positions at Naval Ordnance Test Station (1940s and 1950s), 27; Special Projects Office work, 37, 63; technical director of Polaris program, 54; management approach for Special Projects Office programs, 56, 64, 105; signature authority mandate in SP, 117; promotion to rear admiral, 95

Special Projects Office (SP)
Importance in managing a big research and development project (1950s), 4–5; overall program control and coordination use, 12, 55–57; reorganization into branches (mid 1950s), 55; charter limitations, 57-58; Raborn's personality and management techniques as director (1955-1962), 58–61; coordination and management program developed by Buescher (late 1950s), 62–65; working relationship with contractors, 64, 67–72; focus on ensuring systems interfaced when needed, 65–66; coordination drawings concept initiated by Buescher, 66–67, 72–73; branches, 69; rationale for specific contractor selections, 71; working relationship with bureaus, 72; necessity of complete design control and full-design disclosure requirement, 73–75; staff selection, 74; problems with branches and eventual bypass decision, 75–76; configuration control system at SP-alts to ensure uniformity of the missiles, 77–79, 81; maintenance policy using replaceable modules at SP-alts, 78–79, 86–88; phased installation test program description, 81–83; supervisor of shipbuilding's dual responsibilities, 83; civilian contractor selection system used, 84–86; contractors chosen based on past work and relationships rather than by competitive bidding, 84–86, 124, 126; quality

control and contractor evaluation system description, 89–91; conflicts with DoD over tight quality standards used by SP, 91–92; successful relationship with the fleet due to effective feedback and coordinated project management, 92–94, 100–101; long-term success of quality control and management approach, 92, 96–97, 104, 117; benefits of consistency from low-personnel turnover, 94–96, 104–105; responsibility for training of weapons officers through the Chief of Naval Training, 97–98, 99; trouble and failure reporting systems effectiveness, 100–104; restricted signature authority mandate initiated by Smith, 117–119; Polaris missile project management setup with contractors, 71–72; US-UK Polaris program management and the UK's initiation into SP's coordination and control policies (early 1960s), 106–109; Polaris program management and technical challenges of developing project, 119–121; Polaris development time scale changed from deployment in 1963 to deployment in 1960 due to Sputnik, 122–123; Polaris early test results and repercussions (1958-1959), 123–124; documentation and controlled production processes used to ensure consistency and continuity, 125–126; success due to the dedication and positive attitude of participants in all projects, 126–127; evolution of power interface and numbers deployed decision for the Polaris, 128–130; direct and on-site involvement with the shipyards for Polaris installation and testing (late 1950s - 1960s), 132–135; MIRV development, 137–138; fast pace of programs adopted in response to race with Russian defensive capability changes, 137; US-UK Trident program management (1970s), 107

Sputnik
Soviet launch of this satellite in 1957 shortened the time schedule for the Polaris development program, 122–123

Strategic Systems Programs
See Special Projects Office (SP)

Strategic Systems Project Office
See Special Projects Office (SP)

Submarine-Launched Ballistic Missiles
Polaris (*see* Polaris ballistic missile); Submarine-launched ballistic missile (operational in 1970), 4; MX Peacekeeper development (1980s), 37–38; Trident development and basing decision (1970s), 37, 107, 130, 140; Jupiter development and operational use outside the Navy (late 1950s), 52, 110–112, 122; submarine-launched ballistic missile (operational in 1970), 137, 139–140. *See also* Missiles; Rockets

Talos Missile Program
Surface-to-air missile (developed in 1950s), 32, 80, 81

Teller, Edward
Told Navy that the Atomic Energy Commission could supply a much smaller warhead than that in the Jupiter missile (late 1950s), 112

Terrier Missile
Radar-beam-riding surface-to-air missile (became operational in early 1950s), 32, 57, 80

Torpedoes
Impact of lack of configuration control on torpedo quality in World War II, 15–16; program at the Bureau of Ordnance (mid 1950s), 50–51; look into wire-guided concept by SP, 120–121

Trident C-4 Missile
Metric vs. standard measurement decision (1970s), 37; US-UK joint program management (1970s), 107; development and basing decision (1970s), 130; system designations, 140

United Kingdom
See Great Britain

Vitro Corporation
Help given on Special Projects coordination and management program developed by Buescher (late 1950s), 64, 67–70

VT Fuzes
Development during World War II by Johns Hopkins Applied Physics Lab, 6, 9, 35, 51

Wertheim, Rear Admiral Robert H., USN (USNA, 1946)
Special Projects Office directorship (1977-1980), 55, 69, 94

Withington, Rear Admiral Frederic S., USN (USNA, 1923)
Pride in role in development of Sidewinder missile while chief of BuOrd in mid-1950s, 31

www.ingramcontent.com/pod-product-compliance
Lightning Source LLC
Chambersburg PA
CBHW080612170426
43209CB00007B/1410